HELPING WITHOUT HURTING

IN CHURCH BENEVOLENCE

STEVE CORBETT
and BRIAN FIKKERT

with Katie Casselberry

MOODY PUBLISHERS

CHICAGO

All Scripture quotations, unless otherwise indicated, are taken from the Holy Bible, New International Version®, NIV®. Copyright © 1973, 1978, 1984, 2011 by Biblica, Inc.™ Used by permission of Zondervan. All rights reserved worldwide. www.zondervan.com. The "NIV" and "New International Version" are trademarks registered in the United States Patent and Trademark Office by Biblica, Inc.™

Although scenarios presented throughout the book are realistic or drawn from actual events, names of individuals and churches have been changed.

Crafted for the Chalmers Center by Katie Casselberry
Moody Publishers editor: Pam Pugh
Interior design: Smartt Guys design
Cover design: Faceout Studio
Cover photo of hands holding tablet copyright © 2015 by Warren Goldswain/Stocksy/ 498817. All rights reserved.

Library of Congress Cataloging-in-Publication Data
Corbett, Steve.
  Helping without hurting in church benevolence : a practical guide to walking with low-income people / Steve Corbett and Brian Fikkert.
     pages cm
  Includes bibliographical references.
  ISBN 978-0-8024-1339-0
  1. Church work with the poor. 2. Charity. 3. Benevolence. 4. Poverty--Religious aspects--Christianity. 5. Church finance. I. Title.
  BV639.P6C66 2015
  261.8'325--dc23
                        2015022140

We hope you enjoy this book from Moody Publishers. Our goal is to provide high-quality, thought-provoking books and products that connect truth to your real needs and challenges. For more information on other books and products written and produced from a biblical perspective, go to www.moodypublishers.com or write to:

Moody Publishers
820 N. LaSalle Boulevard
Chicago, IL 60610

1 3 5 7 9 10 8 6 4 2

Printed in the United States of America

PRAISE FOR *HELPING WITHOUT HURTING IN CHURCH BENEVOLENCE*

Just as *When Helping Hurts* served as a road map to help Willow Creek Church shape the strategy of our overall Care Center Ministry, this book will serve as an excellent resource in drilling down a strategy for one of the most challenging topics for church leaders to navigate. Brian and Steve understand the challenges of poverty alleviation yet provide hope through their understanding of God's design for all people.

JOSIE GUTH, Director of Local Outreach at Willow Creek Community Church

Helping the man or woman days from eviction or hours from a power cutoff can be very confusing. *Helping without Hurting in Church Benevolence* will sort out the confusion and guide your church to craft a thoughtful approach to benevolence. Backed by practical experience and thorough research, Steve Corbett and Brian Fikkert show us that it is possible to not only meet an immediate need but also to lead people to lasting change.

JEFF GALLEY, Central Group Leader for LifeGroups and Missions at LifeChurch.tv

This book will undoubtedly be a tremendous tool for churches as they seek to care for the poor with biblical wisdom, sound principles, and pastoral care. In their usual style, Corbett and Fikkert help us to look beyond the surface level requests and to identify and address the deeper issues in the lives of those we seek to serve.

JEFF WARD, Director of External Focus at Watermark Church

Brian Fikkert and Steve Corbett have given the church a practical, adaptable resource for benevolence ministry! This book offers a helpful roadmap that can assist any church to "restore the hope and dignity God intends for His image-bearers." Best of all, it reminds us that benevolence ministry can impact the lives of those in need and those who minister to them, bringing us all to deeper levels of transformation in Christ.

JOHN H. SATHER, Co-national Director of Cru Inner City

Often the most difficult aspect of poverty alleviation is putting good theory into practice. *Helping without Hurting in Church Benevolence* serves as a GPS for converting our good intentions into solutions that give dignity, promote responsibility, and foster lasting change.

STEPHAN BAUMAN, President and CEO, World Relief

I am very happy to see this practical counsel and advice to congregations on how to help the poor. One of the encouragements to me is to see a needed corrective to the first book that Brian Fikkert and Steve Corbett wrote, *When Helping Hurts*, as some churches reading that book may have failed to realize the rich gospel ministry they can experience through needed and immediate relief to people who are in desperate situations. This work helps churches learn how to show mercy with wisdom, and how to walk with people into empowering growth and healing so they can participate in their own development.

RANDY NABORS, Pastor Emeritus of New City Fellowship in Chattanooga, TN, and author, *Merciful: The Opportunity and Challenge of Discipling the Poor Out of Poverty*

When Helping Hurts has become the authoritative road map for all mercy and justice efforts coming out of the church that I serve. This book will no doubt have similar impact as we align our benevolence efforts around the priorities and heart of Jesus.

SCOTT SAULS, Senior Pastor of Christ Presbyterian Church in Nashville, TN, and author, *Jesus Outside the Lines: A Way Forward for Those Who Are Tired of Taking Sides*

Brian and Steve have once again put together a tremendous resource for churches and the body of Christ in this book! As churches, we all struggle with how to best come alongside people with significant needs inside and outside our church. They have given us a very practical step-by-step process to do this well. This is a must read for any church that is helping those in need, which means every church!

PASTOR CHIP SWENEY, Division Director of Next Gen and Community Transformation at Perimeter Church

Serving in a church plant, we have been challenged with developing attitudes and practical strategies for church benevolence on a blank slate. This book does the best job of communicating wise and charitable engagement. It's enriching for any ministry leaders to read together regardless of experience in this area.

JEREMY TAYLOR, Deacon at East Point Church, East Point, GA

Churches are longing for a more fruitful way to address the complex dilemmas that arise in the context of benevolence ministry, and especially among the materially poor. Having used both Chalmers' *Faith & Finances* and *When Helping Hurts* approach extensively in our city, I recognize the ring of truth in the stories here, and the wisdom of the approach.

DR. RANDY WHITE, Director at FPU Center for Community Transformation and author, *The Work of Our Hands: Faith Rooted Approaches to Job Creation, Training and Placement in a Context of Concentrated Poverty*

Finally, it is here! A practical guide for churches to come alongside low-income individuals and families looking for financial assistance. Corbett and Fikkert give excellent guidance through training scenarios and questions, tools, and downloadable forms for churches to "start small, start fast, and succeed."

MARCIA TRANI, Director of Compassion Ministries at Rolling Hills Covenant Church

Caring for and responding to a neighbor requesting financial assistance doesn't have to catch your church flat-footed in how to respond. A flat-out "no" or an indiscriminate "yes" shouldn't be the only two options. *Helping without Hurting in Church Benevolence* provides churches a practical framework. Church leaders will not feel straightjacketed with a recipe approach, but prompted and equipped to develop an approach appropriate to their goals and community.

KIRK VANDER MOLEN, National Director of Missional Integrity at Love In the Name of Christ (Love INC)

The church is charged with a biblical mandate to help the poor in its community. And that includes the responsibility for understanding the underlying causes of poverty. This book offers valuable insights and a practical process to follow.

KIRK LITHANDER, Outreach Pastor at Fairhaven Church, Dayton, Ohio

As a pastor and missions director at our church, we have constantly struggled with having a benevolence process that empowers and builds up the recipient and the helper. *Helping without Hurting in Church Benevolence* gives us the theological framework, structure, and tools to implement a powerful, empowering process.

ANDREW FEIL, Pastor and Missions Director at The Well Community Church in Fresno, CA

CONTENTS

INTRODUCTION

THE MOMENT WHEN . . .

Ben walks through the front door of your church. He approaches the reception desk, explaining that he lives across town and needs help paying his rent. "I've been working real hard at two jobs to take care of my kids," he explains. "But my car broke down this month, and now I can't pay the rent. Can you help me?"

How should your church respond?

Debbie, a single mother who is a member of your church, stops by to visit your pastor's office. She has had a string of jobs over the course of the past year, but just cannot seem to keep one. "I know I said that last month would be the last time, Pastor, but I can't cover my electric bill again this month. I just lost my job because little Emily was sick last week, so I was late to work three days. Can you please help me?"

How should your church respond?

THE SCOPE OF THIS GUIDE

The purpose of this book is to help your church successfully steward the opportunity that arises when someone like Ben or Debbie asks for financial assistance to pay for things such as electric bills, rent, gas, or food. The book guides church leaders, staff, and volunteers through the preparation, interactions, and follow-up work needed to engage in effective poverty alleviation with individuals or households who are seeking such financial assistance. *The ultimate goal is that your church will be better prepared to walk alongside Ben or Debbie in a way that truly helps them and contributes to their being restored to all that God intends for them as His image-bearers.*

Churches describe this type of poverty alleviation using a variety of terms: benevolence work, diaconal work, mercy ministry, or compassion ministry. For the purposes of this book, we will use the term "benevolence" to describe this aspect of a church's poverty alleviation ministry, but it should be noted that churches sometimes use the term "benevolence" in broader ways to include visiting people after a death in the family, walking with people who are mentally ill, or visiting the elderly. Thus, while this book uses the term "benevolence," it is actually addressing only one facet of benevolence work: assisting households who are experiencing material poverty.

This book is not intended to guide a church through all of its poverty alleviation ministries at home and abroad. Rather, it focuses on addressing a specific situation that nearly all churches face: individuals or households asking for money to meet immediate needs. By combining the principles described in our earlier work *When Helping Hurts* with additional research and tools, this book seeks to equip churches to minister effectively in this extremely common situation, bringing positive and lasting change to the lives of low-income people.[1]

Because churches of different sizes vary dramatically in terms of the financial, human, and networking resources they can devote to their benevolence ministries, no single book can address the specific situation of every church. In particular, most small- to midsized churches do not have full-time, paid staff to oversee their benevolence work, while some larger churches do. Thus, although we believe that the principles and tools described in this book apply to churches of all sizes, you may need to adapt them a bit to the specific context of your church and its capacity.

We have written this book primarily for churches in the United States and Canada. It may also be useful for churches in other countries, but they may need to do just a bit more to adapt it for their context. With apologies to our friends in the Caribbean, Central America, Greenland, and Mexico, for the sake of simplicity we use the term "North America" to refer to the United States and Canada.

Finally, although the book focuses on the benevolence work of churches, many parachurch ministries and nonprofit organizations will also find the principles and tools to be relevant and applicable to their context as well.

THE THEORY IS SIMPLE, BUT THE PRACTICE IS COMPLICATED

We have intentionally created this guide to be a streamlined, practical resource, but don't let that fool you: *Poverty is extremely complex, and so is poverty alleviation.*

At its core, poverty alleviation is the process of broken people in a broken world being restored to the hope and dignity God intends for human beings as His image-bearers. And the people who are broken— the people who need this restoration—are *both* the low-income people and those who are seeking to help them. *Both parties are broken, and both need to be transformed.*

But this transformation cannot be packaged into a one-size-fits-all approach. Applying the principles and tools in this book to specific people—specific individuals with unique backgrounds, hopes, gifts, problems, and pains—is necessarily a messy process with all sorts of twists and turns. No amount of principles and tools can completely prepare you to walk alongside the wide range of Marias, Davids, Michelles, Codys, Rosas, Kaitlyns, and Jermaines who approach your church, asking for assistance. Each person is unique, and each church using this guide is unique. As a result, no single recipe or magic formula can be blindly applied to the very wide range of settings.

In addition, because poverty is so complex, the transformation that is at the core of poverty alleviation takes time, lots and lots of time. The restoration of broken people involves the journey of salvation and sanctification that all people—both rich and poor—need to experience over the entire course of their lives.

Although this book attempts to articulate some simple principles, concepts, and tools, none of them can replace the need for the Holy Spirit, prayer, wisdom, and discernment that is at the heart of walking well alongside low-income people. In other words, intellectually comprehending the ideas in this book will not really equip you for effective ministry. Again, poverty alleviation is not simply about applying a recipe. Rather, walking alongside a low-income person requires humbly surrendering yourself in prayer, asking God to give you wisdom, a caring heart, and open eyes as you listen to the person's story. It requires pressing deeper into the good news of the gospel, pleading for Christ's power to fix all that is broken in the low-income person, in you, and in the world in which you both live.

The problems at the root of poverty are complex, so complex that at times you might feel like you just aren't up to the task. In reality, the situation is far worse than this: you are *never* capable of alleviating poverty. Because poverty is rooted in broken individuals and a broken world, poverty alleviation always takes a miracle. The good news of the gospel is that Jesus Christ is in the miracle business every day! Indeed, the Bible teaches that Jesus Christ is reconciling all things in heaven and on earth (Colossians 1:15–20). He is present and active, fixing broken people and a broken world, restoring them to all that He intended them to be.

Our job is not to alleviate poverty! Rather, we are called to be ambassadors of His reconciliation, proclaiming and demonstrating what ultimately only He can do (2 Corinthians 5:18–20). Yes, we are participants in His work, but we are not the authors of that work. We cannot change broken people, nor can we change a broken world. But Christ is in the process of changing both, and He gives us the incredible privilege of being the instruments He uses to accomplish His mission.

DO MORE, NOT LESS!

Following the release of *When Helping Hurts*, many churches retooled their approaches to low-income individuals and communities, moving away from harmful practices and toward more empowering approaches. Unfortunately, some churches became paralyzed and were afraid to help low-income people at all, lest they hurt them in the process of trying to help.

That was never our intention, and it breaks our hearts to hear this!

We long to see more and more churches, ministries, and individuals invest greater time, resources, and energy in helping low-income people. As God's people and as the richest people ever to walk the face of Planet Earth, that is what we are called to do:

If anyone has material possessions and sees a brother or sister in need but has no pity on them, how can the love of God be in that person? Dear children, let us not love with words or speech but with actions and in truth. (1 John 3:17–18)

For the Christian, helping people who are materially poor is not an option. Indeed, as the passage above indicates, our generosity toward the materially poor is one of the primary manifestations that we truly have saving faith.

The point of *When Helping Hurts* is not that you should stop helping materially poor people but rather that you should *do even more* than you have done in the past. Indeed, the reality is that *truly* helping materially poor people typically requires a much greater commitment of time, resources, and energy than the common method of simply giving them handouts. Yes, truly loving people may sometimes mean not offering them material things (1 Timothy 5:3–16), but in no way does this imply that you should do nothing to help them! Rather, it means that you have to look for ways to move away from practices that create dependency and toward approaches that promote long-term positive change.

Unfortunately, due to the complexity of poverty, the best approach or answer is not always apparent. There are moments when you simply do not know what the "right" course of action is. *What if she really can only pay half the rent this month? Maybe his medical expenses really are that overwhelming. Maybe she has tirelessly attempted to find work. What if he really is just trying to travel to visit his ill mother?* In those moments when you have done your best to understand the situation and you still simply do not know what to do, our counsel is to err on the side of giving rather than withholding material assistance. And as much as possible, do this in the context of a long-term empowering relationship that seeks to restore the individual or family to God's design for them as image-bearers.

NOT THE FINAL WORD

Although we have done our best to draw on biblical principles, research, best practices, and our own experiences, we readily admit that this book is not the final word on this important subject. The truth is that there are still many unknowns in benevolence work, so we see this resource as part of a living project, a project that you can speak into as you use this guide. Please let us know what worked well or did not work well as you used this book in your benevolence ministry. You can share encouraging stories and your suggestions for improvement with us at benevolence@chalmers.org.

HOW TO USE THIS GUIDE

This book is primarily designed for church members who directly engage with low-income people on behalf of the church. While each individual engaged in such ministry will find it to be a beneficial resource, it will be most helpful if the church's entire leadership and ministry teams are functioning jointly from the general principles and processes in this guide. Hence, we highly recommend that it be used as a group study to get the appropriate leaders and ministry teams working in concert with one another.

Our goal is to equip you for effective ministry, so this guide aims to be a practical tool kit, not a lengthy treatise:

- Chapters 1 and 2 cover some of the basic principles of poverty alleviation and walk you through some of the complexity of poverty. The goal is to orient you to the realities facing low-income people, preparing you to enter into humble and transformative relationships with them.

- Chapters 3–5 include tools and resources you can use or adapt to guide your church as you walk alongside low-income people. These chapters include shorter modules of content with forms or exercises that are based on materials being used by churches and ministries that are on the frontlines of poverty alleviation on a daily basis.

- Chapter 6 uses a variety of scenarios to enable you to consider what you might do to apply the principles and tools in various situations.

- An online portal contains several resources and tools mentioned throughout these chapters. You can access the portal by creating an account at www.helpingwithouthurting.org/benevolence and entering the access code "walkwith" when prompted.

So let us begin with the hope, prayer, and eager expectation that using this guide will enable us to better help hurting people. And ultimately, may our amazing God—Father, Son, and Holy Spirit—receive praise and worship as our churches embody His love and compassion to broken people and a broken world.

PART ONE

· · ·

A FOUNDATION FOR EFFECTIVE BENEVOLENCE

CHAPTER 1

REFRAMING BENEVOLENCE

UNDERSTANDING THE PRINCIPLES
OF POVERTY ALLEVIATION

As described in the introduction, Ben is struggling to pay his rent, and Debbie needs help with her electric bill.

Those do not sound like enormous problems to solve. But in reality, truly helping Ben or Debbie is usually a very complex process, and there is typically no easy solution. However, there are general principles that can guide you along the way as you walk with low-income people. This chapter describes these principles in order to lay a solid foundation for your church's benevolence work.

It is profoundly important to remember that these principles are not meant to be simple recipes that can be applied blindly to every person. Indeed, the more you delve into any given situation of poverty, the more you are likely to discover all sorts of subtle complexities that require a nuanced approach rather than a one-size-fits-all formula. Hence, understanding the principles in this chapter in no way negates your need to rely upon the *Holy Spirit, prayer, wisdom,* and *discernment* as you walk with low-income people.

Most of the material in this chapter is a brief summary of the ideas presented in chapters 1–6 and 10 of *When Helping Hurts*. Thus, for a deeper understanding of these concepts, you might find it useful to read those chapters as well.

POVERTY AND BROKEN RELATIONSHIPS

Imagine going to the doctor because of chronic headaches. What happens if the doctor diagnoses your problem as a sinus infection when you actually have a brain tumor? Or what happens if the doctor simply gives you a painkiller to treat your symptoms rather than running tests to discover the underlying cause of your headaches? In either case, you are not going to get better. Indeed, you could die from the brain tumor despite the doctor's good intentions. In order for you to get better, it is absolutely essential for the doctor to correctly diagnose the fundamental cause of your illness.

The same is true when we work with materially poor people. Good intentions are not enough. If we misdiagnose the causes of their poverty or treat their symptoms rather than their underlying problems, we can do considerable harm to materially poor people in the very process of trying to help them. We have to get the diagnosis right.

And therein lies one of the fundamental problems with poverty alleviation: being materialistic people, many North Americans tend to think of the disease of poverty as being a lack of material things, such as money, food, clothing, and shelter. As a result, many of us think that the best way to alleviate poverty is simply to give material things to low-income people: money to pay the electric bill, turkeys and toys at Christmas, warm clothing during the winter.

In particular, when a low-income person such as Ben or Debbie approaches our churches asking for help, many of us have a tendency to focus on meeting their immediate material needs by paying their rent or electric bill. Although this is sometimes necessary and can provide much-needed temporary assistance, simply dispensing material resources usually only treats the symptoms of poverty rather than its underlying causes. And if the handouts are repeated over long periods of time to able-bodied people, they can create crippling dependencies. To be truly effective, we need to move past treating the symptoms of poverty—a lack of material things—*and* correctly diagnose its deeper causes.

Toward that end, let's consider poverty from a biblical perspective. God is inherently a relational being. From all eternity, Father, Son, and Holy Spirit exist in perfect relationship with one another. As beings made in the image of this triune God, human beings are wired for relationship as well. Indeed, the Bible teaches that in creation God established four foundational relationships for each human being: relationships *with God, with self, with others, and with the rest of creation*. When these relationships are functioning in the way God designed them to function, humans experience the fullness of life that God intended: we experience deep communion with a loving God; we understand our inherent dignity and worth as image-bearers; we live in positive, giving relationships with others; and we actively steward God's creation, both caring for it and being able to work and to support ourselves as a result of that work. Indeed, when these relationships are working properly, the results bubble up in all aspects of our lives: families are nurturing, communities are flourishing, work is meaningful, and we are bringing glory to God in all that we do.

THE FOUR FOUNDATIONAL RELATIONSHIPS

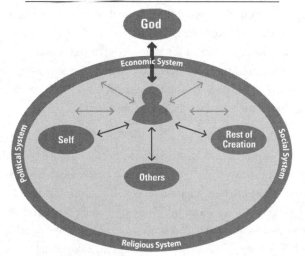

Adapted from Bryant L. Myers, *Walking with the Poor: Principles and Practices of Transformational Development* (Maryknoll, NY: Orbis Books, 1999), 27.

However, the fall has damaged all four of these relationships *for all of us*. How? There are a number of forces at work that undermine these relationships for each person, including the Bens and Debbies who approach our churches asking for assistance:[1]

- *Individual Behaviors* of the person, including their own sins, can undermine the proper functioning of these relationships. For example, if Ben is addicted to alcohol, he may struggle to hold down a job, thereby undermining his relationship to creation.

- *Abusive or Exploitive People* can do severe damage to people. For example, if Debbie's ex-husband physically abused her regularly, those past experiences could still be undermining her self-image (relationship to self), making it difficult for her to work (relationship to creation).

- *Oppressive Systems* (economic, political, social, or religious) can make it difficult or even impossible for these relationships to function properly. For example, a recession can create widespread unemployment, hindering Ben's and Debbie's relationship to creation by undermining their ability to work. Many of us who are not materially poor tend to underestimate the importance of oppressive systems, because by and large the systems have worked well for us. But the systems do not work well for everybody. In particular, the legacy of institutionalized racism—both historic and contemporary—continues to wreak havoc with the lives of many people who are poor in ways that Caucasian North Americans often fail to see.

- *Demonic Forces* are at war with God and human beings as His image-bearers (Ephesians 6:12). Many of us are blind to this cause of poverty, for we North Americans tend to see the world through material rather than spiritual lenses. But Satan and his legions are real and very active, and both the materially poor and the materially non-poor (middle- and upper-income people) need to "put on the full armor of God, so that [we] can take [our] stand against the devil's schemes" (Ephesians 6:11).

For Ben and Debbie, the way that the four relationships are broken results in material poverty, i.e., a lack of sufficient resources to provide for themselves and their families. But this material poverty is a symptom of something deeper: *the underlying brokenness in the four key relationships due to individual behaviors, abusive or exploitive people, oppressive systems, and demonic forces.* Thus, when a person like Ben or Debbie asks your church for assistance, it usually is not enough to *just* address their immediate needs by giving them money, food, or clothing, though such assistance may be appropriate in some situations. Instead, fostering lasting change requires us to move beyond treating symptoms into a much longer-term process of walking alongside them as we all depend on Christ's power to conquer the individual behaviors, abusive or exploitive people, oppressive systems, and demonic forces that are the root causes of their material poverty.

As we engage in this longer-term process of change with low-income people, it is absolutely imperative that we constantly remind ourselves that all of us, regardless of our income level, are profoundly broken and desperately in need of the restorative work of Jesus Christ. Failing to embrace this fundamental truth will typically lead us to inadvertently harm low-income people . . . and ourselves. Indeed, the way that the materially non-poor (middle- and upper-income people) are broken can deepen the brokenness of the materially poor, and vice versa.

To see this, consider how both parties typically experience brokenness in the four key relationships. Among other things, those of us who are not materially poor often experience this brokenness in the form of pride, self-centeredness, workaholic tendencies, and a desire to "play god" in the lives of others. In contrast, materially poor people often experience this brokenness in the form of a paralyzing sense of shame and inferiority, social isolation, and in less than ideal work opportunities and habits.

When the materially non-poor try to help the materially poor, each party brings their respective brokenness into the process. The materially non-poor often exhibit an air of superiority and "play god" by trying to fix the materially poor, thereby confirming what the materially poor are already feeling: "I am inferior; I can't do it; other people need to do it for me." The result is often that the materially poor become more passive, sitting back and waiting for others to fix their problems. And as this happens, the materially non-poor often become more proud: "I knew they didn't have my work ethic and initiative. Why don't they do something to improve their lives?" As a result, the shame of materially poor people is deepened, and the pride of the materially non-poor is enhanced. Both parties end up more broken—more poor in a relational sense—than they were before.

This dynamic is particularly problematic when we have a material definition of poverty. For if poverty is fundamentally about a lack of material things, then we materially non-poor are not broken. We are successful! We have won the game of life! Moreover, we have what materially poor people need: material things. Thus, we are necessarily in the position of being their benefactors, for in our wallets we possess the solution to their problems. A material definition of poverty puts the materially non-poor in a position of superiority over the materially poor.

This common dynamic can be summarized in the following equation:

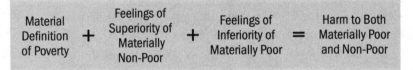

Note that the first two variables in this equation apply to us. Hence, breaking out of this unhealthy dynamic requires us to repent of our trust in material resources and of our sense of superiority. The key is to constantly remind ourselves of the truth of the gospel: *We were all profoundly broken people who deserved eternal punishment; but through Christ's death and resurrection—and absolutely no merit of our own—we are now the adopted sons and daughters of our heavenly Father* (Galatians 4:1–7). Preaching these truths of the gospel to ourselves every day frees us from our pride and enables us to move into a mutually transformative relationship with materially poor people, a context that Christ can use to bring healing to the ongoing brokenness in both of our lives.

Sanctifying Encounters

One morning, the pastor on call asked Eric to join a conversation with a woman who had walked into the church requesting financial assistance. It had been a crazy morning, and Eric, a staff member at the church, jumped into the conversation at full speed. "I started going through my routine of asking questions and looking for information . . . I went straight to logical solutions," Eric explains. She stopped Eric, looked at him, and said, "I'm intimidated by you, and I feel really uncomfortable right now." In Eric's words, "I had missed the most important part: making a heart connection with her."

Eric immediately shifted gears. "I apologized, saying 'Let's slow down, tell me what's going on and how you feel.'" The woman started talking and weeping, letting out the pain she was carrying about in day-to-day life. "I realized she had no one to talk about her life with," Eric says. "Once she felt that relief of sharing her pain, the bills weren't the primary issue anymore. She just got up, and said, 'Thank you for listening and praying with me.' She forgot to even ask for financial assistance."

Eric reflected on this encounter for some time. "I took this experience to the Lord, asking, 'Is this how I am coming across?' That woman worked in my life, leading me to work through my own dysfunction."[2]

Given that poverty is rooted in broken relationships, poverty alleviation can be defined as follows:

POVERTY ALLEVIATION

A process in which people, both the materially poor and the materially non-poor, are empowered to move closer to living in right relationship with God, self, others, and the rest of creation.

The "empowerment" in this definition means that people are growing in their ability to analyze their situation, to make healthy decisions to improve that situation, and to carry out those decisions in all four of these relationships. For example, part of living in right relationship to creation includes their ability to find and perform work that will enable them to support themselves and their families. Ask yourself in each situation: *Will providing immediate financial assistance help or hinder such empowerment?*

THE ULTIMATE SOLUTION TO POVERTY

Given that poverty is rooted in broken relationships, Colossians 1:19–20 is a profoundly important passage for the process of poverty alleviation:

> For God was pleased to have all his fullness dwell in him [Jesus], and through him to reconcile to himself *all things*, whether things on earth or things in heaven, by making peace through his blood, shed on the cross. (italics added)

In this passage, Jesus Christ is described as the reconciler of the entire universe. To reconcile means to put things into right relationship again, restoring them to what God created them to be. Given that poverty is rooted in broken relationships, the fact that Jesus Christ is reconciling all things is truly good news for the poor, a group that includes all of us.

Note that Christ's reconciliation entails more than simply beaming our souls up out of this world into some ghostlike state. On the contrary, Christ is reconciling *all things*, transforming whole people, both bodies and souls. And it doesn't stop there, for Christ is reconciling communities, nature, cultures, institutions, and systems. Yes, He cares about people's souls, but He also cares about hunger, sickness, racism, homelessness, mental illness, spousal abuse, electric bills, and rent payments. How much does He care? Enough to be tortured on a cross so that He could conquer these problems. Jesus cares deeply about Ben's rent and Debbie's electric bill.

It is profoundly important to emphasize that the full benefits of Christ's reconciling work are only for those who repent of their sins and put their faith in Him, while judgment ultimately awaits those who do not. These truths should give us incredible passion to share the good news of the gospel—using both words and deeds—for the gospel is only good news for those who repent and believe.

NOT ALL POVERTY IS CREATED EQUAL

As we seek to bring the good news of Christ's reconciliation to a hurting world, we are immediately confronted with the fact that there are different kinds of material poverty, even though they often look the same on the surface. For example, there is a huge difference between the poverty of a family that cannot pay their rent due to unforeseen health problems and the poverty of a family that cannot pay their rent due to being unwilling to work. The families in both of these situations have a housing problem, but the underlying circumstances that have contributed to their plight are very different and require entirely different responses.

In this light, it is sometimes helpful to think of three broad categories of poverty alleviation:

RELIEF, REHABILITATION, AND DEVELOPMENT

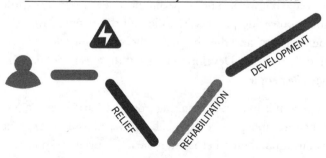

- **Relief** can be defined as the urgent and temporary provision of emergency aid to reduce immediate suffering from a natural or man-made crisis. After a crisis, there is a need to halt the free fall and to "stop the bleeding," and this is what relief attempts to do. The key feature of relief is a provider-receiver dynamic in which the provider gives assistance—often material—to the receiver. Because the needy person is in a crisis, they are typically asked to contribute little or nothing toward reducing their suffering. Although this is not the point of the passage, the Good Samaritan's bandaging of the helpless man who lay bleeding along the roadside is an excellent example of relief applied appropriately (Luke 10:29–37).

- **Rehabilitation** begins as soon as the bleeding stops and seeks to restore people to the positive elements of their pre-crisis conditions. The key feature of rehabilitation is a dynamic of working *with* the person, asking them to take positive actions as they participate in their own recovery.

- **Development** is a process of ongoing change that moves all the people involved—both the materially poor and materially non-poor—closer to being in right relationship with God, self, others, and the rest of creation than they have been in the past. For materially poor people who are able-bodied, development includes their moving toward fulfilling their calling of glorifying God by working and supporting themselves and their families with the fruits of that work. The key dynamic in development is promoting an empowering process in which all the people involved—both the "helpers" and the "helped"—become more of what God created them to be. Development is not done *to* people or *for* people but *with* people.

If a person is in a crisis resulting from a natural disaster, a medical emergency, an unexpected large bill, a physical assault, or some other personal trauma, then relief is often the appropriate response. In these cases, we need to help people quickly and sufficiently to stabilize the chaos that the crisis has created. Although people sometimes need relief repeatedly, it is often the most appropriate response for people who are experiencing a one-time crisis.

But most of the low-income people who approach your church for assistance are probably not experiencing a one-time crisis. They are battling a chronic state of poverty created by a complex set of forces. While they may not be able to change all of the factors that contribute to their situation, if they can contribute something to improving their circumstances, then development—not relief—is the proper approach.

It is profoundly important to note that when using a developmental approach, it might be helpful for your church to provide money or other material resources to the low-income person you are assisting, but you should only do this in a way that builds on the gifts and resources that they are also contributing to their own progress.

Relief doesn't ask people to take actions to improve their situation; development does. Relief is done *to* people or *for* people; development is done *with* people.

Relief says to the family in which the forty-year-old father has a stroke, "Yes, of course we will help you financially until you get back on your feet."

Development says to the person repeatedly asking for help in paying their electric bill, "Yes, we can help you, but only if you are open to exploring with us the reasons you are struggling to pay your bill and to doing what is needed to avoid this problem in the future. Can we help you make the necessary changes in your life?"

One of the most common and detrimental mistakes that North American churches make in their benevolence work is using a relief approach when the situation calls for development. Because we North Americans tend to define poverty as a lack of material things, our churches often give repeated handouts of shoes, clothing, food, or money to people who are not helpless and who are not in a crisis. This approach can deepen the very feelings of shame and inadequacy that are often the root causes of material poverty. In addition, giving handouts, especially repeatedly, can foster a mindset of dependency or entitlement, undermining people's capacity and drive to support themselves and their families through their own work.

Inappropriate Relief: Checking Our Motives

"Even as believers, we might be sinful in our giving. I can give to ease the tension in the room so that person likes me. That's no different than taking shots of whiskey to ease the tension of the day. I'm living in *my* tension, trying to relieve *my* tension."

—**ERIC**, STAFF MEMBER AT EAST RIDGE CHURCH[3]

Of course, knowing exactly when to use relief, rehabilitation, and development is not always clear, for all sorts of added complexities are part of the real world.

For example, your church is not the only option in town. Even if your church believes it is giving financial assistance to Ben "just this one time," other churches and ministries in your community may be doing the same thing for Ben. As a result, your "one-time" gift may actually be just one of a long series of handouts that collectively enable Ben to persist in chronic poverty. If Ben is able-bodied and not in a serious crisis, you should be quick to use creative ways to walk with Ben as he takes actions to contribute to his own improvement (development) and slow to simply give him material resources (relief).

Another complexity is that communities and the individuals within those communities might need different approaches. For example, a community struggling with chronic poverty might need development overall, but some of the individuals or families within that community might need relief, because they are suffering from a real crisis and legitimately need immediate aid.

Furthermore, consider the additional complexity that the same individual might repeatedly move back and forth between needing relief and development. For example, New Hope Church was pursuing a developmental approach with Sarah, a single mother of three who was living in a housing project. New Hope was providing spiritual counsel and discipleship to Sarah, helping her find work and assisting with transportation and childcare. Progress was slow, but Sarah was trying to overcome some of the behavioral issues that had contributed to her material poverty. One day as she was walking home from the store, she was mugged by two men who stole the bags of groceries she had been carrying. The church wisely discerned that while Sarah generally needed development, she also suddenly needed relief. This was not a time to place all sorts of conditions on Sarah before she could get assistance. Sarah and her kids were in a crisis and needed help, so the church bought her several bags of groceries to replace what had been stolen.

Finally, not all low-income people fit the description—at least on the surface—of struggling with a sense of shame or inferiority. Indeed, like many of us, some low-income people struggle with pride and an unwillingness to submit to authority. The key principles and tools in this book still apply to such people, but—as always—you will need to adjust to the particular nature of the people with whom you are walking.

In light of this complexity, here are a few tips:

- Ask the Holy Spirit for wisdom and discernment and then move forward humbly but without fear. Jesus Christ is actively present, and He will accomplish His purposes despite our mistakes. All we can do is our best.

- A helpful rule of thumb is to avoid paternalism: *habitually* doing things for a person that they can do for themselves.[4]

- Don't become paralyzed by trying to categorize people into relief, rehabilitation, or development. When faced with a decision, ask yourself the following question: *If I take this action, will I be contributing or detracting from the long-term goal of empowering this person to live in right relationship with God, self, others, and the rest of creation?*

- When you have done all that you can to discern the best approach but are still in doubt, generally err on the side of providing material assistance.

ASSETS NOT JUST NEEDS

When a person like Ben (or Debbie) walks into your church asking for assistance, what is the first thing that enters your mind? Many of us focus on what Ben is lacking in terms of resources. As a result, we then pursue a "needs-based" approach to working with Ben, focusing on his deficits and needs and assuming that he has little to offer to combat his problems. In this approach, the assumption is that the resources, solutions, and initiative to help Ben will not primarily come from him but from your church. A needs-based approach often exacerbates the very dynamic we need to get out of in poverty alleviation: handing out material resources to people rather than helping them steward and grow their own resources.

In contrast, an "asset-based" approach to walking alongside low-income people starts with the biblical truth that Ben is an image-bearer. Yes, Ben is broken, just as we all are. Yes, maybe Ben is just trying to get the church to give him money he is capable of earning himself. But this brokenness does not negate the fact that Ben retains the image of God and has gifts, resources, and abilities he is called to steward. Indeed, helping Ben become a better steward is one of the key goals of poverty alleviation: seeking to restore people to right relationship to creation. An asset-based approach does not ignore his needs, but it seeks to identify, celebrate, and mobilize his own gifts, abilities, and resources as much as possible to address those needs.

Note that using an asset-based approach does not mean your church should never give resources or other forms of help to Ben, but rather that you should only do so in a way that builds on, not undermines, Ben's use of his own gifts, abilities, and resources. Unfortunately, because we North Americans are materialistic people and because we tend to think that poverty is fundamentally about a lack of material things, we often provide resources too soon and in too large quantities. And in the process, we undermine Ben's use of his own gifts, abilities, and resources.

An asset-based approach can help prevent the unhealthy dynamic captured in the equation mentioned earlier. Focusing on the assets God has given to low-income people frames our interactions with them in light of their God-given dignity and responsibility. It affirms that they have gifts they are called to steward, thereby combating their feelings of inferiority and calling them to take responsibility for improving their situation. This approach also fosters an attitude of respect in our hearts for low-income people, countering our sense of superiority and our tendency to feel we need to fix them.

THE CHANGE CYCLE

Recall that poverty alleviation is a process in which people, *both the materially poor and the materially non-poor*, move closer to living in right relationship with God, self, others, and the rest of creation. Hence, poverty alleviation is fundamentally about change. As mentioned earlier, the changes that are needed often involve addressing individual behaviors, abusive or exploitive people, oppressive systems, and demonic forces. We do not want to downplay the latter two causes, and they will be discussed more in later chapters. But for the moment, let's focus on the first issue. What does it look like for an individual to make the necessary changes in their own behaviors that can help them to emerge from poverty?

Take a moment to reflect on a time when you made significant, positive changes in your own life. What led you to make those changes? Did you ever try to change but fail?

Change does not happen overnight, and making positive behavioral changes is extremely difficult for most people. Indeed, as will be discussed further below, fundamental and lasting change is actually impossible without the saving work of Christ and the power of the Holy Spirit. In addition to this, researchers and practitioners have observed some fairly regular patterns in the way human beings experience change, patterns that can be used to encourage the kind of changes central to the poverty alleviation process.

CHANGE CYCLE FOR INDIVIDUALS

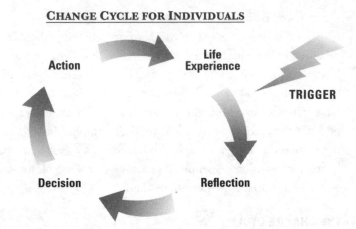

Adapted from David A. Kolb, *Experiential Learning: Experience as the Source of Learning and Development* (Upper Saddle River, NJ: Prentice Hall, 1983).

As pictured above, the context for change is the person's current life experience. Change begins when something triggers this person to reflect on the current situation and think about a possible future situation they would prefer. This reflection can then lead them to make a decision to take some action they hope will move them into a more desirable future situation. Taking this action will lead them to some new life experience. The cycle needs to repeat itself over and over if people are to continue to make positive changes in their lives.

Many different circumstances can serve as triggers for change, but several common triggers that can lead to a desire to change are:

• A recent crisis
• The burden of the status quo becoming unbearable
• Encountering a new way of doing or seeing things that could lead to improvement

One of the key roles your church can play in walking with low-income people is to initiate a trigger for change by gently asking probing questions, introducing new ideas, or helping people see a new set of possibilities. This can lead to a spiraling cycle of action and reflection, a "learning as you go" process: walking with people, trying something *together*; reflecting on the experience, *together*; deciding to try something additional, *together*; reflecting again; trying again.

Of course, once a trigger for change causes some reflection, it is *not* at all automatic that the rest of the cycle will continue. Indeed, a host of obstacles can get in the way of significant change. A major part of the poverty alleviation process is coming alongside low-income individuals to encourage and support them as they remove obstacles in their lives and help them overcome the obstacles they are incapable of removing on their own.

For example, as you and Ben talk about his current financial problem, it might become clear that he needs to think about work differently. So you suggest that he participate in a jobs preparedness program your church sponsors. He decides to give it a try and enrolls in the twelve-week program. As he faithfully attends the classes and attempts to complete the assignments, a member of your church acts as a mentor, helping him with some of the homework, encouraging him, and cheering him on. In the midst of the course, Ben has some financial shortfalls. The mentor lets the church know about Ben's needs, and the church helps pay a few bills as a way of supporting Ben on his journey. Ben graduates and soon gets a job due, in no small part, to the great references from his mentor and the course instructors.

RECEPTIVITY TO CHANGE AND PARTICIPATION

Of course, change is only possible in a low-income person if he or she is willing to change. If Debbie does not believe that change is possible, if she is unwilling to go through the pain of change, or if she does not believe that she is the person who is primarily responsible for making the necessary changes in her life, it will be very difficult to make progress with her. Indeed, one of the most challenging elements of poverty alleviation is identifying those people who are truly ready to change: namely, those who have experienced a trigger for change and are willing to embark on the process of change. Chapter 4 will discuss the use of an "intake form" as a tool to gauge a person's receptivity to change. Remember: while we have a crucial role to play in the life of a low-income person, we cannot effect change. Rather, our role is to be an encourager of them as they initiate and drive their own change process.

In order for a low-income person to pursue the hard road of making the necessary changes in his or her life, it is profoundly important that they own the course of action from the very beginning. This means that Debbie must see herself as the person who is primarily responsible for making these changes happen. Like most human beings, low-income people generally own plans that they have helped to initiate and to shape more than plans that have been imposed on them.

Hence, poverty alleviation efforts should avoid "blueprint" approaches that impose a predetermined plan on a low-income person with our ideas about what to do and how it should be done. A blueprint approach fails to create the necessary ownership of the change process that is essential if the low-income person is going to initiate and sustain the necessary changes in their life. In addition, a blueprint approach tends to exacerbate the harmful dynamic in which the materially non-poor "play god," speaking and acting in ways that confirm the sense of inferiority and shame that many low-income people are already feeling.

In contrast, a participatory approach asks Debbie what she believes she should do to improve her life, how she thinks she should do it, and what actions she will take to pursue positive change. This does not mean that you should never speak into Debbie's life but simply that you act in a way that is consistent with biblical truth. As an image-bearer, Debbie has insights and abilities, and she is called by God to be the primary person who stewards those insights and abilities by using them to initiate and sustain positive changes in her life.

THE LOCAL CHURCH AND POVERTY ALLEVIATION

We have described an asset-based, participatory process that moves in a developmental direction because we believe it is a powerful approach to fighting poverty. However, the concepts and principles we have discussed must be rooted in something deeper: the power of Jesus Christ to address individual behaviors, abusive or exploitive people, oppressive systems, and demonic forces that cause the broken relationships that are at the heart of poverty. And this is where the local church has far more power in her than first meets the eye. The Bible teaches that the church is the body, bride, and fullness of Jesus Christ, the only one who can truly alleviate poverty (Ephesians 1:18–23; 4:7–13; 5:32). The poor need Jesus Christ, the reconciler of all things, and He is found in the local church!

The Church as Family

"I think churches haven't sized up their gifts. We are not a bank, we are a family. I drive you to the doctor; I don't perform the surgery myself. I help you get a bank account set up; I don't give you the money. I put my family hat on in this work. Family doesn't fix your car; we help you get the car fixed. [This framework] invites relationship . . . What would a family do? I don't need to solve everything!"

—JAMES, DEACON AT NEW LIFE CHURCH[5]

Dear brother or sister, you may often feel inadequate and overwhelmed as you work with your church's benevolence ministry. But take heart, for you are not alone! The triune God is working in and through you and your entire church. As people are drawn into the fellowship, life, and worship of your church, they encounter Jesus Christ Himself! In fact, even just the "ordinary" activities of the church that we so often take for granted—the preaching of the Word, baptism and the Lord's Supper, accountability and discipline, and prayer—are the very means that God has *ordained* to draw people into a saving relationship with Jesus Christ and to be nurtured in that relationship.[6] These routine things work! They accomplish God's purposes, not because your church is so talented but because God has declared that these are the means that He ordinarily uses to draw people into a saving relationship with Jesus Christ and to nurture them in that relationship.

And as we mentioned earlier, this relationship with Jesus Christ is the foundation for addressing all the causes of poverty for believers:

- We are made into new creatures in Christ and are given power by the indwelling Holy Spirit to embark on the painful and slow process of addressing the *individual behaviors* that contribute to all of our poverty (2 Corinthians 5:17; Ephesians 4:17–32).

- We get to celebrate Christ's conquering of *abusive or exploitive people, oppressive systems,* and *demonic forces.* We see some of this happening now, but we also wait in eager expectation for that great day when His kingdom will be fully consummated (Revelation 21:1–7).

This relationship with Jesus Christ is not just something abstract and theoretical. Rather, it is experienced—yes imperfectly, but really—in the family of the local church, a family that consists of the adopted sons and daughters of our heavenly Father (Galatians 3:23–4:7). Indeed, when someone from either inside or outside your church seeks assistance, you have something to offer them in addition to rent money or food. You get to offer them a nurturing and supportive family that embodies in its words, actions, and life together the reality—in the here and now—that Jesus Christ is indeed making all things new by conquering the individual behaviors, abusive or exploitive people, oppressive systems, and demonic forces that impoverish all of us in various ways.

Think about it: your benevolence ministry is often the front door through which people enter into this incredible family!

CHAPTER 2

TAKE A SECOND LOOK

RECOGNIZING THE COMPLEXITY OF POVERTY

As described in the introduction, Ben is struggling to pay his rent, and Debbie wants help with her electric bill.

Recognizing that these immediate needs are just symptoms of deeper issues, your benevolence team offers to pursue a longer-term developmental approach with them. As it does so, it encounters numerous ups and downs along the way. In fact, sometimes it is hard to know if you are even making any progress.

Ben responds positively to your offer of a long-term relationship. So a member of your benevolence team works with him on a budget, and they come up with a plan that seems viable. Because the plan requires Ben to make some difficult lifestyle changes in order to reduce his expenditures, Ben agrees to meet with somebody from the church on a weekly basis for the purposes of accountability and encouragement. So Derek, a volunteer from your church, meets Ben for lunch each week, and they seem to be developing a good friendship. Until the fourth lunch meeting . . .

The meeting starts out as always: they order their meal, engage in small talk about sports, and joke with the waitress. After asking the blessing over the food, Derek casually says, "Hey Ben, I keep forgetting to ask you how you are doing on your budget. Have you been able to stick with it?" Ben's demeanor suddenly changes; he jumps up and shouts, "Who do you think you are? Get out of my face! All you do is criticize me!" Ben storms out of the restaurant, leaving Derek dumbfounded and embarrassed by the stares of other diners.

Progress with Debbie is up and down as well. She seems particularly comfortable with Ashley, a member of the benevolence team, so the two of them meet to create an action plan. As will be discussed in chapter 3, an action plan is a statement of the person's goals and of the steps they will take to achieve those goals. As they develop the plan together, Debbie, who is normally very outgoing, suddenly gets a distant, dazed look on her face and stops talking. It is almost like she is not fully present. After a while, Debbie abruptly leaves without saying a word. Ashley texts and calls Debbie for the next several weeks with no response.

What is going on in these two situations? It is entirely possible that Ben's and/or Debbie's behavior indicate they are not really interested in making lasting change. Perhaps they are just trying to get money out of your church and are getting frustrated at how long it is taking. But there are other possible explanations as well.

As described in the previous chapter, poverty is rooted in relationships that are broken due to the following factors: (1) individual behaviors; (2) abusive and exploitive people; (3) oppressive systems; and (4) demonic forces. The first factor is internal to the person, while the latter three factors are external. In reality, the internal and the external factors are often highly interconnected. As a result, while we may be tempted to simply blame Ben or Debbie for their actions, we should also be aware of the external factors that may be contributing to those actions. There may be more going on with Ben and Debbie than meets the eye.

Considering how these external factors may be contributing to Ben's and Debbie's behavior does not mean that they are not responsible for their own actions. On the contrary, sin is sin, and people do have to take responsibility for their actions even when there are contributing external factors. But having a greater awareness and understanding of these external factors can help us in at least three ways as we seek to walk with low-income people:

1. *Avoiding Wrong Conclusions*: We might be too quick to interpret Ben's and Debbie's behavior as meaning that they do not really want to go through the long-run process of change. As a result, we could give up on them too easily.

2. *Moving from Frustration to Empathy*: When people engage in behaviors that undermine their progress or are manipulative or offensive, we naturally get frustrated with them. Sometimes just a bit more understanding of the "cards they have been dealt" can help us be a little more patient as we walk with them.

3. *Offering More Effective Help*: As we better understand some of the complex causes that contribute to people's behaviors, we are able to design and implement more effective benevolence ministries.

With those ends in mind, this chapter gives just a glimpse of some of the external factors that may be contributing to the behaviors of Ben and Debbie.

THE EFFECTS OF ABUSIVE OR EXPLOITIVE PEOPLE: A GLIMPSE INTO THE WORLD OF TRAUMA

Working with Ben and Debbie would be frustrating to any benevolence team. In fact, most people would be angered by Ben's outburst. But if we consider Ben's and Debbie's childhoods, things might start to look a bit different.

Ben was a fantastic baseball player as a boy. Hitting, fielding, throwing, baserunning—he could do it all so naturally. Dave, Ben's father, had played minor league baseball, and scouts said Dave had a chance to make it big in the major leagues. But once Dave suffered a serious back injury, and he was done. Unable to cope with the disappointment, he turned to alcohol to suppress the pain.

Ben looked absolutely adorable in his Little League uniform, but he was never smiling in any of the old pictures. He always had an intense look on his face. It looked as though he was carrying the weight of the world on his shoulders . . . and indeed he was. For whenever Ben made a mistake—striking out, failing to make a catch, or throwing high—things got ugly at home. Dave would go into a drunken rage, screaming at Ben and whipping him with his belt. Several times Ben had to be rushed to the emergency room because of the injuries he sustained.

You want to hug the little boy in that uniform, protect him, and make his pain go away. You do have that chance, for that little boy is now thirty-five years old and he is shouting at you—or perhaps at his father—"Who do you think you are? Get out of my face! All you do is criticize me!"

When Debbie was a little girl, she spread joy everywhere she went. Her pigtails, smile, and outgoing personality endeared her to every adult she encountered. Uncle Joe particularly relished spending time with Debbie, finding ways to be alone with her, gaining her trust with gifts and treats. Unfortunately, the relationship turned abusive: Uncle Joe sexually molested Debbie from the time she was eight until she ran away from home at the age of sixteen. Embarrassed and horrified, Debbie never reconnected with her family.

Again, you want to hug that little girl and protect her from all harm. But now she is an adult and is hiding from you, refusing to answer your phone calls and texts.

Ben and Debbie both experienced trauma, which can be defined as an event, a series of events, or a set of circumstances in which a person feels physically or emotionally harmed at a level that is greater than their capacity to cope; as a result, the event(s) or circumstances have lasting, negative effects on the person's functioning and overall well-being, effects that can last a lifetime.[1]

Not every low-income person who seeks assistance from your church is suffering from trauma, and not every person who experiences trauma becomes materially poor. But it is likely that some of the people asking you for assistance have experienced trauma, for trauma can be both caused by and contribute to material poverty. For example, studies have found the following:

- 88 percent of homeless mothers report having experienced severe physical and/or sexual violence at some point in their lives, with 42 percent reporting sexual abuse in childhood;[2]

- 83 percent of inner-city youth report experiencing at least one traumatic event;[3]

- 60–90 percent of youth in the juvenile justice system have experienced trauma.[4]

At the time of the traumatic event(s) or circumstances, the person experiencing the trauma has intense feelings of fear, horror, vulnerability, helplessness, and loss of control, which they typically respond to by fighting, fleeing, or freezing.[5] How the trauma then affects the person for the rest of their life depends on a host of factors, including biological makeup, personality, socioeconomic status, and the extent to which they have loving families and social networks.[6]

Although the long-term effects vary by person, many trauma survivors who later encounter situations that remind them of their initial traumatic experiences can be "retraumatized," causing them to react in the same ways that they did when the traumatic events actually occurred. In particular, because many people experience trauma at the hands of people who are close to them—a parent, spouse, sibling, relative, friend, or caregiver—getting close to the new "caregivers" on your benevolence team can be especially frightening for them.

For example, when Derek asked Ben if he was sticking to his budget, it may have reminded Ben of his father's criticism and abuse, thereby causing Ben to fight back. Similarly, as Debbie was growing closer to Ashley, it may have triggered painful memories of the close relationship that Debbie once had with Uncle Joe, a relationship that became abusive. As a result, Debbie responded to Ashley the same way that she responded to Uncle Joe as a child: emotionally distancing herself from the experience and then running away and hiding.[7]

Indeed, as your benevolence team works with trauma survivors, it could trigger all sorts of behaviors and emotions, including:[8]

- withdrawal and avoidance
- dependency
- shame
- self-injury
- alcohol and substance abuse
- aggressive acting out
- vacillation between being highly emotional and completely un-emotional
- controlling of others
- loss of self-control
- contradictory behaviors
- reactivity

Unfortunately, these types of behaviors often lead to social isolation for trauma survivors, as they reject people or are rejected by them. The loneliness that results from this isolation eventually causes the trauma survivor to crave deep human relationships. As a result, trauma survivors often swing back and forth between being fiercely independent and being intensely dependent upon others.[9] So while Ben and Debbie are hiding from your benevolence team right now, next week they could be demanding all of your attention. These fluctuating and volatile behavior patterns create special challenges for your benevolence team and volunteers, requiring large amounts of patience, understanding, and wisdom.

How can your benevolence team minister effectively to people who have experienced trauma? While it is beyond the scope of this book to make you experts on trauma care, here are a few tips:

- Be aware that trauma could be affecting some of the people who are asking your church for assistance. Some of the behaviors you are observing—even some of the most aggravating ones—could be evidence that this person has experienced trauma. If so, it is likely that the person is not even fully conscious of all of the behaviors they have adopted. Ask God to help you to move from frustration to empathy.

- Consider the possibility that the person's behaviors are a valiant attempt to cope with a horrendous situation. Instead of seeing all their behaviors as intentionally hurtful to themselves and others, be open to the possibility that this person is simply trying to survive a highly painful set of events or circumstances.

- Be aware that your attempts to help the person could actually be retraumatizing, triggering all sorts of emotions and behaviors. Be patient, understanding, and steady as the relationship goes through various ups and downs.

- Avoid actions that are retraumatizing. A significant step in this direction is giving the person a strong sense of control and empowerment throughout the process. Because a loss of control and vulnerability are at the heart of the horror of trauma, it is extremely important that your engagement with trauma survivors gives them a sense of being in charge, empowering them to use their own gifts and abilities to manage their own process of change.[10] The good news is that this is exactly what the asset-based participatory approach in this book is designed to do for everyone who asks your church for assistance. However, if you become aware that the person has experienced trauma, be even less directive than usual, bending over backward to give the person a very strong sense of being in charge: *When would you like to meet? What works for you? You've done incredibly well at navigating some very difficult circumstances! You are amazing! What do you think is the best way forward?*

- If the person you are assisting is suffering from the long-term effects of trauma, you may want to provide financial assistance more quickly than you would otherwise. Doing so can lessen the vulnerability and anxiety that they are feeling about the unpaid bill, buying you some time to be able to work through longer-term issues with them.

- If the population you are serving includes a large number of people who have been affected by trauma, you may want to get additional training on trauma-informed care for your benevolence team, volunteers, and church.

- Recognize that your benevolence team is unlikely to have all of the expertise it needs for assisting people who have experienced trauma. Chapter 5 discusses the need to access existing services in your community, and one of those services needs to be centers with professionals trained to help with trauma recovery.

We should not lose sight of the fact that long-term trauma is just one of the many negative impacts of abusive or exploitive people. For example, if a husband beats his wife, he could inflict serious short- and long-term physical damage on her apart from the long-term psychological effects of the trauma. And when an employer abuses his or her workers through verbal threats, physical harm, inhumane working conditions, and unjust wages, the worker immediately suffers economically, physically, and emotionally, in addition to the long-term psychological impacts of the trauma.

THE EFFECTS OF OPPRESSIVE SYSTEMS: ENVIRONMENT MATTERS

As discussed in chapter 1, the fall of humanity into sin has affected everything in the universe, including the cultural systems (economic, political, social, and religious) humans create. As a result, systems that should enable human beings to flourish often do the exact opposite.

For example, we all felt the effects of a broken economic system during the Great Recession that began in 2007–2008. Many people lost their jobs, causing them to have a broken relationship to creation. Broken systems are indeed a contributor to poverty. While the Great Recession had a significant impact, for many North Americans the effects were not devastating. Yes, it was very difficult to be laid off and to see stock values plummet. But the economy has rebounded, and many North Americans continue to enjoy a standard of living that is unprecedented in human history.

But not all broken systems have such transitory effects. Sometimes broken systems have very long-lasting and deep effects, inflicting harm that spans generations and that drives right down into the very neurons in their victims' brains. Indeed, it is entirely possible that some of Ben's and Debbie's behaviors may have to do with the long-term effects of oppressive systems in their lives, systems that they did not choose to be born into . . . systems that none of us would choose to be born into.

Again, sin is sin, and Ben and Debbie are responsible for their own actions. But understanding how oppressive systems may be contributing to those actions can help us avoid drawing the wrong conclusions about Ben and Debbie, move from frustration to empathy, and interact with them more effectively.

A Tale of Two Americas

In *Our Kids: The American Dream in Crisis*, Robert Putnam documents how key changes in the past fifty years—increasing income inequality, a breakdown in community, and shifting cultural attitudes about marriage and sexuality—have combined to create two separate Americas.[11]

The first America is characterized by rising income and wealth, safe neighborhoods, good schools, opportunities for advancement, and often two-parent families that invest considerable time and money nurturing their children.

The second America is characterized by stagnant or falling income, neighborhoods that are increasingly fragmented and violent, inferior schools, and dysfunctional families that are often less than nurturing.

Putnam finds evidence that these two Americas are increasingly isolated from each other, both geographically and socially. As a result, children in the United States are often born and reared in different realities—almost two distinct countries. The first "country" provides ever-increasing opportunities, while the second "country" seems to trap people into multigenerational poverty.

Why the entrapment? Many factors are at work, but we will focus on three features of the environment of the second America that may be contributing to Ben's and Debbie's behavior.

First, a growing body of research is demonstrating that the environment and experiences of early childhood—especially prenatal through the age of five—dramatically affect the development of the brain and nervous system, having results that last through adulthood. In particular, children who are born and raised in the highly stressful environment of the second America are likely to develop brains with underdeveloped "executive functions"—i.e., *the ability to solve problems, cope with adversity, organize their lives, and exhibit self-control*—which inhibits their ability to function for the rest of their lives.[12] Although it would take further exploration, some of the behaviors of Ben and Debbie are consistent with a loss of executive functions.

Second, the most important feature of a young child's environment is their parents. Research is finding that positive physical and verbal interactions between parents and young children is crucial to healthy brain development, which in turn has lifelong effects on their intellectual capacity, emotional stability, physical health, and self-control. Unfortunately, many parents in the second America are able to provide less nurturing than parents in the first America. One study found that by the time they entered kindergarten, the children of professional families in the first America had heard 32 million more words than the children of parents on welfare.[13] Similarly, parents with professional degrees annually give about 166,000 verbal encouragements and 26,000 verbal discouragements to their children, while parents on welfare give an average of 26,000 encouragements and 57,000 discouragements.[14] While we do not know much about Debbie's upbringing, Ben's was certainly less than nurturing.

Third, a growing body of research suggests that the highly stressful environment of *low-income urban neighborhoods* can cause trauma. Economic strain, violence, discrimination, illness, family dysfunction, and overall instability combine to create effects that are similar to the trauma caused by abusive or exploitive individuals we saw earlier.[15] In other words, even if Ben's father had not beaten him and Debbie's Uncle Joe had not sexually abused her, they still might be exhibiting the behaviors associated with trauma simply from growing up in the highly stressful environment of a low-income urban neighborhood.

The Ongoing Effects of Racial Discrimination

In addition to the general effects of growing up poor, we have the additional legacy of racial discrimination in America. Most readers are already somewhat familiar with America's history of discrimination against African-Americans, Native Americans, and some other minorities. Reviewing these histories can help to increase our empathy as we walk with low-income people who have suffered from this reality.

We need to keep two more important points in mind.

First, racial discrimination is not just part of America's past; it is an ongoing problem. Though our culture has improved in this respect, there is evidence that racial discrimination is still a fact of life for many in such diverse areas as employment, health care, housing, the justice system, and even in online sales. Indeed, the problem of discrimination is amazingly difficult to erase. Researchers are finding that even when people are not consciously prejudiced, they still subconsciously engage in discriminatory actions that do real—albeit unintended—harm to racial minorities.[16]

Second, a racially discriminatory environment has effects that drive deep inside its victims. Researchers are finding that systemic racism actually rewires the brains of those who are being discriminated against, causing them to *automatically* think, feel, and act in ways that are consistent with the system's racist messages. In other words, those who are being discriminated against start to unconsciously believe that they really are an inferior race, that they really are incapable . . . that they really are whatever the racist system says they are.[17] If Ben or Debbie are from a racial minority, they may be dealing with issues that are foreign to some of us.

THE EFFECTS OF DEMONIC FORCES: UNSEEN BUT REAL

While it is difficult to know how demonic forces might be at work in any specific situation, it is important to continually remind ourselves that those forces are very real and are actively waging war against people (Ephesians 6:10–18). This fact never removes Ben's or Debbie's responsibility for their own actions and sins (Genesis 3; James 1:13–15).

However, being aware of Satan's active presence reminds us that there is a larger drama at work in their lives and in our benevolence ministry, and that we need to constantly pray for protection and deliverance for everyone involved.

JESUS IS BIGGER

While we have only touched on the external forces that may be contributing to the behaviors of Ben and Debbie, you are probably already feeling overwhelmed! In fact, you might even be feeling a bit discouraged. Take heart. Yes, many internal and external factors may be dragging Ben and Debbie down. But as discussed in chapter 1, Jesus Christ is far bigger than any of these problems. Thus, we can put our trust—not in our money, techniques, or wisdom—but in the fact that Jesus Christ really is making all things new.

PART TWO

· · ·

DESIGNING AND IMPLEMENTING AN EFFECTIVE BENEVOLENCE MINISTRY

CHAPTER 3

BUILT FOR TRANSFORMATION

CREATING A BENEVOLENCE PHILOSOPHY AND POLICIES

Articulating a thoughtful philosophy and a set of concrete policies for your benevolence work is the first step in preparing to assist people like Ben and Debbie.

If your church does not take the time to develop a philosophy and policy document, your benevolence ministry will lack the compass it needs to keep moving in the right direction. Soon the scope and scale of the requests for assistance could overwhelm you and pull you away from accomplishing your primary objectives. This chapter walks you through a series of questions to help you develop a philosophy and set of policies that can keep your benevolence work focused, intentional, and effective.

Prayerfully work through these questions with your benevolence team in order to develop a final document that you can all own as you move forward together in ministry. If you already have a document that articulates your current benevolence philosophy and policies, you will want to keep it in front of you as you work through this chapter. It may already address many of the questions posed below, so you can use this chapter to confirm, adapt, or expand your current philosophy and policy document.

Although you should carefully construct your philosophy and policies, do not agonize over getting them perfect the first time around. Recognize that you are going to have to learn as you go, especially if you are making significant changes from how you have historically engaged in your benevolence ministry. It is better to have an imperfect document that gets you moving than spending countless months unable to act while you wordsmith a document that will need to be modified anyway.

Below is a set of questions that you should answer as you create or revise your benevolence philosophy and policies. You can also download these questions by following the instructions at the end of the chapter. The remainder of the chapter provides further explanation and guidance to help you answer each of these questions.

TOOL 1—DEVELOPING YOUR CHURCH'S BENEVOLENCE PHILOSOPHY AND POLICIES[1]

DEVELOPING YOUR BENEVOLENCE PHILOSOPHY
Focusing Our Purpose: What Are We Trying to Accomplish?
1. What is the problem to be solved? In particular, what is poverty?
2. What is the goal?
3. How will we try to achieve our goal?

DEVELOPING YOUR BENEVOLENCE POLICIES
Focusing Our Ministry: Whom Will We Help?
1. How do we prioritize those seeking assistance?
2. Do we have a special opportunity with a specific target group?

Focusing Our Resources: What Type of Help Will We Give?
3. What percentage of the benevolence budget will be used for relief and what percentage will be used for development?
4. Are there any types of assistance we will not provide?
5. How often and how much will we consider giving to people in various categories?

6. How will we respond to people who are capable of working but who are unwilling to work full-time?
7. How will we seek to incorporate all adult household members in the process of assistance and long-term change? Specifically, how can we honor and uphold family units—including the relationship between husbands and wives—in the intake and action plan process?

Focusing Our Process: What Procedures Will We Follow?

8. How will we design the intake process?
9. When will we not require an intake form to be completed in order to receive assistance?
10. What sort of fact-checking will we do?
11. When will we not require an action plan to be completed?
12. When and how do we want to utilize other ministries or agencies?
13. Will attending church and/or listening to an explanation of the gospel be required in order to receive any assistance?
14. What will we do to address abusive or exploitive individuals who may be contributing to the person's poverty?
15. What will we do to address oppressive systems that may be contributing to the person's poverty?
16. What will we do to address the demonic forces that may be contributing to the person's poverty?

Focusing Our Message: How Will We Share and Solidify Our Guidelines?

17. How will we publicize our policies to the church?
18. How will we publicize our policies to the community?
19. Are there other items we should address in our policies?

DEVELOPING YOUR BENEVOLENCE PHILOSOPHY

Your benevolence philosophy is a brief statement that captures the overall approach you will use to helping people like Ben and Debbie. This philosophy statement needs to embody your basic DNA, i.e., your foundational convictions about what you are trying to accomplish and how you will get there. You will use this philosophy both to shape your standing policies and to guide you in making wise decisions in each particular situation.

FOCUSING OUR PURPOSE: WHAT ARE WE TRYING TO ACCOMPLISH?

Your benevolence philosophy should answer these three basic questions:

1. What is the problem to be solved? In particular, what is poverty?

As described in chapter 1, the way we define the causes of poverty profoundly shapes the solutions we use to alleviate poverty. For example, if we believe poverty is fundamentally due to a lack of material things, our approach will focus on giving material things to low-income people. If we misdiagnose the causes of poverty, our approach will not be effective and could actually do harm. It is essential we get the diagnosis right.

As summarized in chapter 1, it is consistent with a biblical framework to think of poverty as being rooted in the broken relationships each person has with God, self, others, and the rest of creation. These relationships are broken due to some combination of the individual's own behaviors, abusive or exploitive people, oppressive systems, and demonic forces. If you are in agreement with this framework, you might want to adopt it as your own by putting it into your own words, elaborating on certain points, and contextualizing it for your specific situation. For example, if your church is in a context in which predatory lenders are oppressing people through deceptive lending practices, you might want to explicitly mention this as something to be addressed in your ministry.

2. What is the goal?

The first step in achieving a goal is to state it. For many North Americans, the goal of life in general and of poverty alleviation in particular is to achieve greater consumption of material things. This goal has a profound effect on the approach many North Americans take to working with poor people.

As described in chapter 1, the biblical view of human flourishing involves far more than simply consuming more material things. Instead, the Bible indicates that human beings are called to be image-bearers of the triune God. In this light, the goal of poverty alleviation is to empower both the materially poor and non-poor to move closer to image-bearing: living in right relationship with God, self, others, and the rest of creation. For able-bodied people, this includes their being able to glorify God through work that enables them to support themselves and their families. If you are comfortable with this framework, you might want to adopt it as your own by putting it into your own words and by contextualizing it for your specific situation. For example, if your church is in a community in which divorce rates are high, you might want to specify that you would like to intentionally address the broken relationships between husbands and wives in your community in order to promote healthier marriages and families.

The Goal: Thinking Beyond a Check

Rose approached James's church, New Life, with the goal of gaining assistance with her rent. Instead, she found a long-term community.

Rose said her husband was in prison, and her son was deployed with the military. She worked hard at her part-time job, but couldn't get enough hours to cover her financial needs. She was too embarrassed to ask her son for help, insisting, "I would hate for my son to see his mom this way."

James, a deacon at New Life, was sensitive to Rose's situation. But instead of focusing on the rent bill, James told her, "We try to concentrate our financial assistance on those who are a part of our fellowship. We've found it is hard to really help folks we don't know. Will you let us get to know you better?"

James invited her to *Faith & Finances*, the financial education and discipleship class that his church hosted every week. In the class, Rose found a supportive community, learned money management skills, and explored biblical stewardship principles. After graduating from the class, she joined a jobs preparedness class to support her in her job search.

Rose is still trying to find a job with more hours, but she is now stewarding her limited income more carefully. She has also shared her financial struggles with her son, removing an emotional barrier in their relationship.

In the meantime, she has become an active part of the church. "She comes to church every week, spends time with my wife, and is an absolute joy to be around," says James. "She will even call me on things, saying, 'Mr. J—there you go with all that talk. You gotta listen more!'"[2]

3. How will we try to achieve our goal?

You should articulate a few key principles that will guide you as you seek to address the causes of poverty in order to achieve your goal. For example, how will you address the individual behaviors, abusive or exploitive people, oppressive systems, and demonic forces that cause the broken relationships? As described in chapter 1, Jesus Christ is the key to addressing all of these contributors to poverty, so your key principles should be centered on using His power as the ultimate source of change.

For example, your key principles might look something like the following statements:

- *Because humans are relational beings, we will seek to provide material assistance in the context of long-term empowering relationships.*

- *Because Jesus Christ is the ultimate solution to poverty, we will seek to enfold people as full participants into His body, i.e., our church family.*

- *Because the goal is restoration to image-bearing, we will use approaches that build on people's own gifts, resources, and abilities.*

TASK TO COMPLETE: Adopt a Benevolence Philosophy Statement

Using the three questions above, create your benevolence philosophy statement or revise your existing one. Then get the statement approved by the appropriate leaders in your church. Keep it brief—several para-

graphs should be sufficient. You certainly need to spend time ensuring that you have a solid vision for your church's benevolence work, but do not agonize over every word to the point where you get bogged down or frustrated. Just put together a basic philosophy that unifies your church leaders and volunteers around a common vision for benevolence. Remember that after some time and experiences, you will undoubtedly update your philosophy in light of what you have learned, removing some portions, clarifying ideas, or going deeper in particular concepts.

DEVELOPING YOUR BENEVOLENCE POLICIES

Once your benevolence philosophy is defined, you can create policies that bring your philosophy to bear on your actual practices. This is where the rubber starts to meet the road, so it is important that you carefully try to articulate policies that will enable you to minister most effectively.

Why Policies?

"When someone in need comes here, there is an expectation that they will get material things from us. We have guidelines we follow, and that helps us in the hard conversations. We can say, 'According to our guidelines, this is what we can do.'"

—ERIC, STAFF MEMBER AT EAST RIDGE CHURCH[3]

The primary goal of benevolence policies is to give a concrete basis for decision making to those who are on the frontlines of your benevolence ministry. They are the people who will be faced with the difficult task of making wise decisions about the best ways to help Ben or Debbie. Although no set of policies can provide your benevolence workers with the answers to every situation, a clear set of policies can provide them with the guidance they need to keep your benevolence ministry focused and effective.

In addition, such policies can protect your benevolence workers from having to be the "bad guy" all the time, enabling them to say, "I am sorry, but our church's policies do not authorize me to provide funds for that type of request."

Moreover, such policies can empower your benevolence workers to be the "good guy," enabling them to say, "You are asking us to write you a check, but we are eager, willing, and prepared to provide you with so much more. We want to work with you toward a long-term solution to your situation."

As you create new policies or adapt your current ones, remember that *the purpose of benevolence assistance is to support and encourage low-income people to improve their lives, building on their own actions, gifts, and resources.* Run every sentence or guideline you create through that filter. As you try to specify the situations in which you will provide material assistance, remember that the goal is to see materially poor individuals taking steps to improve their own lives and the lives of their families, participating in their own change as they move toward being in right relationship with God, self, others, and the rest of creation. Of course, such improvement ultimately rests on the power of Christ's death and resurrection and on the indwelling Holy Spirit to effect fundamental and lasting change.

FOCUSING OUR MINISTRY: WHOM WILL WE HELP?

1. How do we prioritize those seeking assistance?

If a person is in real danger of physical harm and your church is in the best position to assist them, you should always give them the highest priority. But beyond that extreme situation, it is helpful to prioritize people for getting assistance of various kinds from your church. Will you help only church members? What about friends of members? Are you only willing to help people from the church's neighborhood? Will you take referrals from other churches or organizations? What about those who just drop in off the street?

Such prioritization might sound callous, given that every person is created with equal dignity and worth as an image-bearer. However, prioritizing different categories of people can help your church to engage more deeply with those whom you are truly positioned to help. Because poverty is deeply rooted in broken relationships, lasting and sustained progress usually requires a longer-term, focused effort, not a quick-fix, shotgun approach. Hence, given limited human and financial resources, determining where your resources can truly make a lasting difference is part of sound stewardship.

Although we are to express Christ's love and compassion to all people, the Bible does indicate that our first priority is to assist fellow believers (Galatians 6:10). Moreover, the Bible is clear that such assistance is to extend beyond the local congregation into the global network of churches (2 Corinthians 8–9). Depending on how your church is structured, this sharing of resources with other churches that are in need may come out of your missions budget, your benevolence fund, or some other place. Although this book focuses on how your church can minister directly to the Bens and Debbies who are asking your church for assistance, if this interchurch sharing of resources is to come out of the benevolence fund, you will need to determine how to prioritize this item and the percentage of the budget to allocate to it.

When it comes to the funds that your church will spend directly on the Bens and Debbies who are asking your church for assistance, you should prioritize people who are engaged with your church body in some capacity over those who are completely unknown to you. Your congregation is in a good position to accurately ascertain the assets and needs of such people and to provide them with the support, encouragement, and accountability that they need. This does not mean that you should exclude others from receiving any assistance, but it does mean that you should prioritize the needs of your own members and of those who are under the auspices of your church's ministry in some way.

Related to the previous paragraph, you should prioritize those who are expressing and demonstrating receptivity to making lasting changes in their lives. Chapter 4 describes an intake process designed to provide an initial gauge of people's receptivity to change, but such receptivity also needs to be evaluated throughout the entire process of walking with people over time.

In setting your priorities, you may also want to consider geographic boundaries. Members of North American churches often reflect very large geographic areas, as attendees frequently gravitate to churches that mesh with their theological positions and personal preferences rather than those in their own neighborhoods. If your church is open to providing benevolence assistance to all of your attendees' friends, neighbors, or relatives, your church could find itself writing checks to people with whom you have very little capacity to enter into the long-term relationships that are at the heart of poverty alleviation.

For these reasons, some churches emphasize a sense of "place" in their benevolence work, choosing to focus on serving people in the immediate community surrounding the church. For my (Steve's) church in a rural setting in Georgia, the immediate "community" covers a large number of miles, and we do not receive many requests from outside that area. But if your church is located in a more urban setting, you should consider defining a more precise geographic region. Typically, churches with tighter geographic focus have a greater impact over time, as they repeatedly bear witness to Christ's restoration in a specific neighborhood or community.

2. Do we have a special opportunity with a specific target group?

Consider whether there is a target group your church is uniquely called and equipped to assist, such as young children, single parents, the elderly, or refugees.

First, look at the makeup of your community and the people who are already asking for assistance from your church. Do not lose sight of their assets, but do you see any common patterns in the needs they are expressing? For example, are people struggling with educating their children? Or is there a high immigrant population in your neighborhood that frequently needs help to get on its feet?

Next, does your church seem particularly gifted in addressing any of these common needs? For example, do you have former teachers who would be interested in starting an after-school tutoring program? Or do you have people gifted in teaching English as a second language? Chapter 5 describes asset mapping, an approach to consider using to identify and mobilize the gifts in your congregation.

If you find that your church seems to have gifts for addressing the needs of a particular population, your church might have an opportunity to develop a specific ministry to serve them. You might want to prioritize the participants in such a ministry for benevolence assistance, since you are in a better position to develop long-term relationships with them. If other churches and agencies refer people to this ministry, will you, as a general rule, provide benevolence assistance to such referrals?

FOCUSING OUR RESOURCES: WHAT TYPE OF HELP WILL WE GIVE?

3. What percentage of the benevolence budget will be used for relief, and what percentage will be used for development?

As discussed in chapter 1, *relief* is the urgent and temporary provision of emergency aid to reduce immediate suffering from a natural or man-made crisis. Relief can range from assisting someone whose house has burned down to providing immediate shelter and resources for a woman experiencing domestic abuse. *Development* is a process of ongoing change that moves all the people involved—both the materially poor and the materially non-poor—closer to being in right relationship with God, self, others, and the rest of creation than they have been in the past. Development expenditures might include subsidizing counseling for somebody who has experienced personal trauma, providing childcare while a person gets job training, or helping someone purchase a suit for a job interview.

Because relief is a response to a crisis, it is inherently unpredictable. It is impossible to know when a tornado might rip through your community or when a family in your church might face massive medical bills in the wake of a car crash. However, despite this uncertainty, we still recommend that you allocate a portion of your benevolence fund for *relief* and another portion for *development*.

Why? As discussed in chapter 1, one of the most common and detrimental mistakes that North American churches make in their benevolence work is using a relief approach in situations that call for development. Because we North Americans tend to define poverty as a lack of material things—and because development work is so difficult and time-consuming—our churches often give repeated handouts of shoes, clothing, food, or money to people who are not helpless and who are not in a crisis. We need to protect our benevolence work from this predisposition, and one way to do this is to put a ceiling on the amount we are going to spend on relief, thereby encouraging ourselves to move more toward development.

Unexpected Types of Assistance

Nate, a church staff member at Grace Fellowship, encounters a range of financial requests in their downtown community. While a significant portion of their ministry involves referring people to specialized organizations in the area or entering into long-term development relationships, they encounter some unexpected forms of one-time assistance.

For example, many young people—especially women with children—come to the city looking for work or to stay with friends and family. "They don't know what to expect, and they often find themselves in a far worse situation than what they left to come to the city," explains Nate. "If someone is trying to get back home to a better situation, our church and other community service agencies will split the bus fare to get them back to that more stable environment." In the process, Nate and his church help remove these young people and women from vulnerable situations.[4]

The percentage of money you should allocate to relief or development depends on the needs and existing resources in your particular community. However, in most places in North America, the vast majority of low-income people need development, while the existing organizations and ministries are often focused on relief. In this light, we generally recommend that the majority of your benevolence budget should be devoted to development, not relief. Again, such an allocation does not mean that you will never help somebody with food, an electric bill, or rent, but simply that in most cases such assistance should be provided as part of an overall development process that is building on people's own gifts, resources, and abilities.

Of course, if the number of legitimate crises in a year exceeds the amount of funds allocated for relief, the benevolence funds can be re-allocated. However, this reallocation should require the approval of a committee with higher authority, such as the elders or deacon board, than any individual who is on the frontlines of benevolence work. This higher authority should determine if the situation really involves a cri-sis that is worthy of reallocating funds away from the longer-term de-velopment that most poor people need . . . and that we are often the most hesitant to provide.

4. Are there any types of assistance we will not provide?

You are likely to receive a wide range of requests for help, so it is helpful to decide in advance any type of assistance that you will not provide. Do your best to set this policy upfront, but you may need to revisit the issue down the road as you gain experience with the types of requests that are commonly made by the people in your context.

We suggest that you *never provide assistance in the form of cash.* Keep gift cards to a local grocery store on hand, make payments straight to a utility company, and directly communicate with a local auto mechanic to assist with any car repairs.

Some benevolence ministries also refuse to pay for such things as "rent-to-own" electronics, cable television, and luxury items.

You might also decide not to offer certain types of assistance that are already being provided by others in your community. For example, if an agency or service already provides assistance with electric bills, you might choose not to provide such assistance yourself. In this case, you should determine the best way to link this existing service to your benevolence ministry. This does not mean that you should simply re-fer people to another service, but rather that you will use the service as part of your overall process of walking with the low-income person over time. Chapter 5 discusses the creation of a Community Resource Directory in which you will document the types of services that are already available in your community.

In the process of working with low-income people, you may need to learn about types of expenses that are foreign to your experience, such as payday loans. Low-income people often do not have emergency funds set aside or access to traditional forms of credit. When they are in a financial crisis, they often turn to payday loans, high-cost loans that must usually be repaid in full within two weeks. Frequently, the borrower will not be able to pay back the initial loan, so they end up rolling it over again and again, paying additional borrowing fees each time. A large-scale study found that the average person in the United States who takes out a payday loan rolls it over ten times, paying $458 in fees on an initial loan of $350, trapping the borrowers in debt.[5]

Payday loans are just one of the sources of credit that are commonly used by low-income people. There are also car-title lenders, mortgage brokers, rent-to-own stores, tax refund creditors, and pawnshops, all of which charge very high interest rates and can bury people in a cycle of debt. Do not underestimate the importance and impact of helping someone to pay off these expenses, but do so only as part of a long-term development process in which you are helping the person learn how to avoid these kind of loans in the future.

As they try to solve the problem of these high-interest lenders, some churches are tempted to offer low-interest loans to materially poor people. We generally advise against this approach. It is very difficult for churches to enforce loan repayment by seizing collateral or by other means. This failure to enforce loan repayment teaches irresponsibility and can result in widespread defaulting once people learn that the church is not serious about enforcement.[6] In addition, churches have reported that people who fail to repay their loans are often too embarrassed to ever return to the church again. If a person is in great need, we recommend a gift rather than a loan. And if the goal is long-term financial development, you can find other ways to help people build wealth besides loans, including financial education and Individual Development Accounts, which are matched savings programs for low-income people.[7]

5. How often and how much will we consider giving to people in various categories?

How many times per year will you be willing to give assistance to the same individual or family? Is there a maximum amount of help per year?

These benchmarks will differ for relief and development situations, but one of the goals in both relief and development is to move people toward living in right relationship with creation by being able to support themselves through their own work. Hence, your policies and decisions should try to avoid creating unhealthy dependencies that undermine this overall goal.

Relief situations should typically involve one-time aid. Assisting with rent or utility bills multiple times in a year without that person truly committing their own time, energy, gifts, and resources to an overall process of change is generally a bad practice.

In development situations, the frequency of the assistance will vary. People in the development process might have financial needs multiple times in a year, but any assistance you provide should be in the context of the long-term process of change. Your assistance might be needed to fill financial gaps multiple times along the way, but such assistance must complement people's use of their own gifts, abilities, and resources to improve their lives. If there is no evidence that people are taking action to use their own gifts, abilities, and resources, you may need to withhold assistance to avoid enabling them in persistence of unfaithful stewardship.

Again, it may be necessary to make exceptions to the policies you adopt. But such exceptions should be made by a committee with a higher level of authority than the individual who is on the frontlines of the benevolence ministry.

6. How will we respond to people who are capable of working but who are unwilling to work full-time?

Some people are unable to work full-time, or sometimes even part-time, due to significant mental or physical disabilities; others are simply unable to find work due to a lack of available jobs. But if a capable person simply chooses not to work at a "normal" level in order to provide for themselves and their families, it is unbiblical and harmful to provide financial assistance to them (2 Thessalonians 3:6–15; 1 Timothy 5:3–16). Sometimes people will say that they do not want to work because the work is too hard or too menial or because they do not like the workplace environment. Unless the person is too physically or mentally impaired or the workplace is dangerous or abusive, these reasons do not justify being willfully unemployed or underemployed. You need to encourage the person to work and then also help them to improve their skills and abilities so that they can obtain "better" work.

7. How will we seek to incorporate all adult household members in the process of assistance and long-term change? Specifically, how can we honor and uphold family units—including the relationship between husbands and wives—in the intake and action plan process?

As much as possible, all of the household members who are contributing to its income and expenses need to be on board with any plan for making positive, long-term change, as all their attitudes and actions will impact whether or not the plan is successful. Hence, the more that you can bring all of the relevant people—spouses, adult children, or cohabiting adults—into the process, the better.

Many churches see a pattern of husbands wanting to remain on the fringes in the process of asking for assistance and creating an action plan, whether out of pride, shame, or passivity. People both inside and outside the church hold a wide range of opinions about the roles of men and women in the family. Thus, you will need to carefully consider what fostering healthy family dynamics, particularly the relationship between husbands and wives, looks like for your context and for each household that approaches you. Two issues are at play:

First, in situations in which a wife approaches the church for assistance, we believe that as heads of their households, husbands should not be let off the hook in the process of planning and committing to change. They need to show leadership in taking responsibility for their family, so you should do your best to bring the husband into the conversation as soon as possible. However, as you do so, you need to show great concern for how the wife is feeling, ensuring that she does not feel confused or belittled by your deliberate efforts to involve her husband. This would be an excellent time to assign a married woman from your benevolence team or church to be the point person for walking with the wife who is presenting the request for assistance. Further, you must be sensitive to the situation that she is in, which could be abusive. In these cases, contacting her husband could put her in danger, and you will need wisdom to ensure her safety, in addition to providing any financial assistance.

Second, because cultural values continue to change with respect to the definitions of "family" and the roles of husbands and wives within a family, this area needs particular sensitivity, especially when dealing with unbelievers. While the church must always uphold God's standards for family and marriage, it must do so out of a nonjudgmental, gospel-centered humility. You need to start with where each family and marriage is at in its understanding of God's design, and as you walk with them over time, the opportunities for sharing the good news of the transforming power of Jesus Christ will be numerous.

FOCUSING OUR PROCESS: WHAT PROCEDURES WILL WE FOLLOW?

8. How will we design the intake process?

The first step of the intake process involves communicating when and where people can submit a formal request for assistance. Can they begin the process by calling the church office? Can they walk in and begin the process immediately? Or will they be directed to come back to the church at a specific time to meet with a particular volunteer or staff member?

The intake process should utilize two key tools: (1) an intake form and (2) an action plan.

The intake form gathers basic information about the person's identity, contact information, background, and current situation. Gathering this information helps you determine whether or not to assist the person, the type of help they need, and how receptive they are to long-term change. In addition, at the end of the year you can look back over these records to get a sense of the kind of help you gave and the results you have observed in order to determine any adjustments you want to make for the upcoming year. Chapter 4 helps you to create and use an intake form.

As described in chapter 1, walking with people developmentally requires that they commit to a longer-term process of participating in their own change. As part of the intake process, you should work with the person to create an asset-based, participatory action plan that helps them to set their own goals, identify their abilities and resources, commit to taking steps to improve their lives, and describe what your church will do to support them in the change process. A person's willingness to complete an action plan with you is one gauge of their receptivity to change. Chapter 4 helps you create and use an action plan.

*9. When will we **not** require an intake form to be fully completed in order to receive assistance?*

While you will use the entire intake form in most situations, there may be times when you choose to use only part of it or to forgo it initially.

For example, if a man walks into your church and says that his electricity will be cut off in four days, using the full intake form is generally both feasible and appropriate. The man has time to complete the form, and unless extremely hot or cold weather are factors, his electricity being shut off for a brief period of time will primarily be an inconvenience. However, if a woman asks for help because she and her children are in immediate and serious danger, having her fill out a lengthy form and asking her numerous questions about her situation is not the appropriate response in that moment. In such a situation, you should just get the woman's name, address, and contact information and then proceed to help her to resolve the crisis.

In addition, it might be necessary to develop a deeper relationship with the person before they are willing to answer all of the questions.

For example, not everybody will be ready to disclose all their financial matters on the first visit, and it may take a long time before people are willing to talk about their emotional and mental health issues. In particular, as discussed in chapter 2, people who have experienced trauma may flee when they have a sense that they are losing control in a situation. If the person becomes agitated or suddenly expresses the need to leave, you could warmly invite them to return whenever they are ready to complete the form with you. Alternatively, you might decide to skip some portions of the form until much further down the road in your relationship with the person.

Your policies need to outline the situations in which the entire intake form needs to be completed, and those situations in which portions of it can be delayed or even skipped altogether.

10. What sort of fact-checking will we do?

You will need to determine your standard procedure about the level of fact-checking that you will routinely require. Some churches have a policy to take people's stories at face value, choosing to simply trust the information people provide on the intake form. But there are ways to corroborate a person's story to help you discern how to use your limited benevolence funds. In addition, as will be discussed further in chapter 4, fact-checking is an opportunity to get a more complete picture of the person and their situation in order to be able to help them more effectively.

Due to increased federal and state legislation with respect to privacy and confidentiality, you should consult with a lawyer to determine the parameters for sharing and obtaining information. In some states, it may be advisable to ask the person seeking assistance to sign a form that waives their rights to privacy.

Consider the following options for fact-checking a person's story:

• *References*: Make follow-up calls to references provided in section 1 of the intake form in chapter 4. Recognize that their friends will most likely support their story. But it is still a good step to take. Sometimes you can sense through the phone call to what degree the story is complete and accurate.

- *Other Churches and Agencies*: The intake form in chapter 4 asks whether or not the person is receiving any other help from local churches or agencies. You can call the other churches or agencies listed to confirm the details provided on the intake form. Similarly, if someone approaches you for assistance with a bill, call the company or landlord to gain a sense of the payment history and to ensure that the bill reflects the current balance.

- *Community Databases*: Some communities have databases in which churches and other charitable organizations can record information about whom they have assisted and what type of assistance they have provided. This allows you to track whether a person has received repeated financial help or whether they failed to disclose assistance from another church in the intake process. Such databases prevent people from receiving aid from church after church,

Why Check the Facts?

Fact-checking does not require launching a weeklong investigation. It can be as simple as a phone call. Nate, on staff at Grace Fellowship Church, shares a story of when fact-checking paid off. An unemployed gentleman requested assistance on his $170 electric bill. Nate glanced at the information, and everything seemed fine. "I will often delay making a commitment and a decision," Nate explains. "I will simply say, 'Everything looks pretty good—I will get in touch with you,' so I can dig a bit deeper." He called the utility company, and discovered that the majority of the bill had been paid already. "If I had written a check, I would have been giving him future credit. So I contacted him, and said we could not help [financially] because he hadn't been forthright and honest with us." Nate's church was willing to walk with the man over time in the development process, but by withholding immediate financial assistance, they made it clear that honesty would have to be a component of that journey.[8]

thereby "gaming" the system and taking advantage of churches' generosity. This does *not* mean that you should refuse to help an individual just because they show up in a database as having received assistance from another church or agency. Rather, it gives you a glimpse of the person's history and honesty and enables you to collaborate with others in ministering to this person most effectively. One such database that your community might want to use is called Charity Check (www.charityck.com).

*11. When will we **not** require an action plan to be completed?*

You will use an action plan any time you are engaging in development. In relief situations in which you are providing one-time assistance to a person in a crisis, an action plan is likely not needed.

While an action plan should always be completed in a development situation, it does not need to be completed all in one sitting. Indeed, inherent to the development process is helping people to identify and mobilize their gifts, abilities, and resources in order to embark on a long-term process of change. Giving people time to think about their assets and how they will use them to improve their lives is actually part of the development process and need not be rushed. In addition, if the person is dealing with trauma, it may be too threatening for them to complete the entire action plan in one sitting. Move at their pace, allowing them to have a sense of control throughout the process.

12. When and how do we want to utilize other ministries or agencies?

In benevolence work, you will often encounter people who are experiencing challenges that are beyond your church's ability to address. For example, your church likely will not have all of the skills and resources needed to help somebody struggling with severe substance abuse or with long-term trauma. However, your community might have service agencies that specialize in helping people overcome these obstacles, and you can help people to access these agencies' services.

Having a list of the organizations and services available in your community can prepare you to help people with the challenges that your church cannot address on its own. Chapter 5 guides you through the process of creating a listing of these community agencies and services. For now, consider the common needs you know your church cannot meet.

Note that your goal is not to simply refer people to other agencies and ministries and then walk away. Rather, the goal is to develop a longer-term empowering relationship with the people asking you for help. While you may need to utilize the services of other organizations, you will want to walk with low-income people before, during, and after they use those services, providing them with the spiritual, emotional, and financial support they need in order to make lasting changes in their lives. The action plan you will create with the person should include the services that will need to be accessed from other organizations, thereby incorporating these services into the overall plan of walking together in an empowering relationship.

13. Will attending church and/or listening to an explanation of the gospel be required in order to receive any assistance?

There is a real difference between encouraging benevolence workers to look for opportunities to communicate the truths of the gospel and requiring the people whom you are assisting to attend your church. Different churches take different approaches to this question. Your church leaders should discuss this issue and help you to formulate a policy that is consistent with their overall philosophy.

Although good people can disagree on this matter, it is our view that it is best to avoid mechanical or perfunctory approaches in which people are simply going through the motions to satisfy the conditions of receiving assistance. At the same time, we believe that those working in a benevolence ministry should be actively and creatively looking for opportunities to verbally share the gospel and enfold people into the life of the local church. For as discussed in chapter 1, ultimately only Jesus Christ can reconcile the broken relationships that are at the heart of poverty, and people receive Christ by hearing the good news of the gospel (Romans 10:14–15).

14. What will we do to address abusive or exploitive individuals who may be contributing to the person's poverty?

Much of benevolence work focuses on addressing the individual behaviors that are contributing to the person's material poverty. However, as discussed in chapter 1, many low-income people are also the victims of abusive or exploitive people such as spouses, relatives, friends, landlords, employers, or lenders. In some cases, even the police or the criminal justice system can mistreat people. It is not possible to create a set of policies that will be sufficient to address every situation. However, you should note that you are likely to encounter this situation at some point, particularly with respect to abusive or exploitive spouses, relatives, and friends. Talk to the police department, your local government's department of family services, and any agencies that deal with domestic violence to determine the best course of action, including how you should work with them to resolve such situations.

15. What will we do to address oppressive systems that may be contributing to the person's poverty?

As discussed earlier, oppressive systems—both past and present—can also dramatically contribute to poverty.

While we cannot change the past, developing a greater understanding of historic injustice and its lasting effects are important to helping all of us to develop greater patience with low-income people. In addition, asking the person seeking assistance about any family history with respect to injustice and truly listening with an empathetic heart can contribute to their healing and to developing deeper trust with one another. In fact, a failure to listen and empathize will often prevent you from being able to truly walk together in a trusting relationship.

In addition, as you work with people over time, you should be on the alert for oppressive systems that may be currently contributing to people's poverty. Is the school system providing satisfactory education in your community? Are adequate jobs available? Affordable housing? Are fair banking services obtainable for low-income people? Is the health-care system serving low-income people? Although it is unlikely that your benevolence ministry has the capacity to tackle these issues, your benevolence workers are often well positioned to identify the systems that are wreaking the most havoc in people's lives. Your benevolence ministry can then bring these oppressive systems to the attention of the church's leadership and congregation as a whole. This can then lead to other parts of your church body seeking to address these wider systemic issues.

16. What will we do to address the demonic forces that may be contributing to the person's poverty?

Satan is at war with God, which puts him at war with human beings as God's image-bearers (Ephesians 6:10–12). Since the inability to fully experience image-bearing is at the core of poverty, Satan is pro-poverty. He has a vested interest in attacking poor people and any ministry that seeks to truly help them.

In most cases, the people seeking assistance from your church will not recognize that demonic forces could be at work. Indeed, most of us in North America tend to forget that Satan is very active in the world and is seeking to harm us.

What should you do? The Bible says that we are to "put on the full armor of God" in order to resist Satan's schemes: truth, righteousness, the gospel, faith, salvation, the Word of God, and prayer (Ephesians 6:14–18). You should carefully consider how you will incorporate these into your benevolence ministry, but here are a few suggestions.

Specific prayers for God's protection and transforming power should surround all aspects of your benevolence ministry. For example, you might want to consider the following:

- Benevolence teams and volunteers praying with every person who asks your church for assistance;

- Benevolence teams praying over each action plan during regular meetings;

- Volunteers praying in the adjacent room while a financial education or jobs preparedness class is being offered;

- Visitation teams praying in the homes of those receiving assistance.

In addition, one natural way to incorporate the Word of God is to provide relevant training on such things as financial stewardship or jobs preparedness using curricula that intentionally integrate the Scriptures. Chapter 5 discusses two such curricula that are available from the Chalmers Center (www.chalmers.org): *Faith & Finances* and *Work Life*.

FOCUSING OUR MESSAGE: HOW WILL WE SHARE AND EXPAND OUR GUIDELINES?

17. How will we publicize our policies to the church?

Once you have created these policies, communicate them to people in your church so they know what to expect from your church's benevolence ministry. Conflict can erupt if someone in your church expects assistance that is outside of the bounds of your policies. Satan loves conflict, and he will find every place that he can to create tension and disunity in the body of Christ. Thus, be sure that the church body knows the policies and some of the basic reasons for having these guidelines. Place flyers in the church foyer, post them on your website, and make them easily available in your church office.

18. How will we publicize our policies to the community?

People outside your church who might approach you for assistance also need to understand the basic guidelines. This *does not* entail spelling out every policy and every detail. It *does* mean having posters or short brochures that communicate how you are willing to help people—and what will be required of them. I (Steve) am familiar with a church that posts their policies right next to the entrance to their offices. Many times people walk up, look at the policies, and then just walk away. I have often wondered if some of those individuals thought, "This church is too serious. I can't get easy help from them. I don't want to bother." While the goal of posting policies is not to scare people away, doing so communicates that receiving assistance from your church requires time and commitment. As a result, it increases the likelihood that people who do go through the intake process will be receptive to change.

19. Are there other items we should address in our policies?

If you have items in your current policies you want to keep, or other things you want to address, you should incorporate them as well. You do not want your policies to be so long and complicated that no one can understand them. But you do want to ensure that they reflect the experiences, wisdom, and concerns of your benevolence workers.

TASK TO COMPLETE: Adopt a Set of Benevolence Policies

Using the questions above, create your benevolence policies document or revise your existing one. Then get the document approved by the appropriate leaders in your church. Although you should carefully construct your policies, do not agonize over getting them perfect the first time around. Recognize that you are going to have to learn as you go, especially if you are making significant changes from how you have historically engaged in benevolence ministry.

One of the principles of poverty alleviation is start small, start fast, and succeed.[9] The same applies to your church's ministry. Let creating your benevolence philosophy and policies serve as an energizing foundation for your work, not as a discouraging obstacle. Get moving, refusing to let perfectionism get in the way of taking your first steps in walking with people like Ben and Debbie.

EXPLORE ONLINE RESOURCES

Create an account on the Chalmers Center's User Portal to access some of the tools and resources mentioned in this chapter.

Create an Account At:
www.helpingwithouthurting.org/benevolence

Enter Access Code: walkwith

CHAPTER 4

FROM ELECTRIC BILL TO RESTORATION

WALKING WITH PEOPLE
THROUGH A CHANGE PROCESS

By creating a benevolence philosophy and policies, you have laid the foundation for focusing your benevolence work.

When Debbie or Ben approach your church for assistance, you are no longer starting from scratch; you have a defined purpose and a set of policies to guide your interactions, and you are now ready to embark on an empowering approach with them. This chapter describes this process, focusing particularly on the early stages in which a solid plan must be established in order to foster an ongoing dynamic of positive change.

Before describing this process, keep in mind three important points.

First, this process is not meant to be a one-size-fits-all formula to mechanically follow. Each individual who asks your church for assistance is unique, and both you and your church are unique. You must use prayer at each step along the way, asking the Holy Spirit to give you the wisdom and discernment you need in order to truly help the person asking for your assistance.

Second, many of the individuals approaching your church are members of families. They often have spouses, children, and other dependents, all of whom may be contributing to the problem and all of whom may need to be part of the solution. While for the sake of simplicity this book often uses language about "the individual" or "the person" asking for assistance, do not lose sight of the fact that walking with this individual often means walking with their entire family. In particular, if the person has a spouse, it is usually the case that this spouse will need to own and participate in the process of change if it is to be successful.

Third, the status of your heart as you interact with Debbie or Ben is far more important than any detail in this process. As discussed in chapter 1, we must always operate out of a gospel-centered humility, reminding ourselves that we too are broken and need Christ's ongoing work in our own lives. We need this gospel-centered humility to avoid being condescending, to be a good listener, and to express warmth and patience. And we need this gospel-centered humility to transparently share our own struggles with Debbie or Ben, opening up our own hearts to them and to what God might want to teach us throughout this process.

A Call to Humility

"Don't forget that you might be the client. God might have sent that person to sanctify you."

—ERIC, STAFF MEMBER AT EAST RIDGE CHURCH[1]

The early stages of the process are centered on the use of two tools: (1) an intake form and (2) an action plan. This chapter provides examples of these tools and discusses their use. In addition, you can download these tools by following the directions at the end of this chapter. But remember, these tools are just suggestions. You should adapt them to the particular context of your church and community.

THE INTAKE PROCESS

The intake process with Debbie or Ben starts with asking questions in order to complete some or all of an intake form. A sample intake form is below, followed by further explanation and guidance for each of the sections. We have adapted and expanded it with permission from the *Diaconate Manual* of Redeemer Presbyterian Church (PCA) of New York City.

TOOL 2—INTAKE FORM[2]

Date Notified_____ Response Call_____
Intake Completed_____ Actual Interview_____

SECTION 1: Identifying Information

Name:_____
Age _____ Male _____ Female _____ Couple _____
Address:_____
_____
Work phone:_____ Home phone: _____
Cellphone:_____
Email:_____
Spouse's name:_____
Children's names and ages:_____
_____
_____
Family members living with person: _____
_____
Church member? _____yes _____no   If yes, how long? _____
If no, regular attender? _____yes _____no   If yes, how long? _____
If not a regular attender, is this person connected to the church in any way?
_____
Has this individual been previously assisted by the church?
_____yes _____no
If yes, when?_____

What was the help for? _____

What help was given and to what degree? _____

_____

_____

Did the individual receive financial assistance? _____yes _____no

Has this individual received assistance from other churches/agencies in the past year? _____yes _____no If yes, what was the help for? _____

_____

What help was given and to what degree? _____

_____

_____

List names and phone numbers of personal/pastoral references who could be contacted for further information regarding this individual (ask for verbal permission to contact these references): _____

_____

_____

SECTION 2: Current Situation and Reason for Request

What is the presenting problem as stated by the individual? _____

_____

_____

_____

_____

How long has this problem been going on? _____

_____

Has the individual recently been victimized by abusive or exploitive people in ways that have created/contributed to the problem? _____

_____

_____

Has the individual done or not done anything that has contributed to the problem?

_____

_____

Other important details of the situation: _____
_____
_____
_____
_____
_____

What steps has this person taken to remedy the situation?_____
_____
_____
_____
_____
_____

What is the individual's specific request of the church? _____
_____
_____
_____
_____

What does this person think needs to be changed in the situation and/or in themselves? _____
_____
_____
_____

Is this person willing to work with the church to create an action plan aimed at solving their current problems as well as working to help prevent this problem from occurring again?_____
This form was started by:_____
on (date) _____
Person assigned to follow up:_____

SECTION 3: Detailed Context and History

You may want to wait until future meetings to obtain some or all of the following information. Use your judgment.

Be sure the person requesting help is told of the information they will need to provide, including documentation as needed, to complete the intake form.

Education/Work History

Current job held: _____

How long at present job?_____

Work history: _____

_____

_____

_____

_____

_____

Highest level of education and degrees held:_____

_____

_____

Other training certificates or programs completed: _____

_____

_____

_____

_____

Financial Position[3]

MY MONTHLY SPENDING PLAN			
MONTHLY INCOME	Current Income	Income Changes	New Budget
Employment (Take-home pay—after taxes)			
Government Assistance/ Unemployment			
Pensions/Retirement			
Child Support/Alimony			
Friends/Family			
Social Security/Disability			
Food Stamps			
Other:			
Other:			
TOTAL INCOME			

MONTHLY EXPENSES	Current Expenses	Spending Changes	New Budget
Housing (Rent/Mortgage)			
Electricity			
Gas			
Water			
Telephone (Home/Cell)			
Cable TV/Internet			
Laundry Costs			
Groceries			
Snacks/Drinks/Cigarettes			
Medicine/Prescriptions			
Household (Toiletries, Cleaning, Cooking)			
Pet Food and Supplies			
Childcare/Child Support/Alimony			
Meals Out/Entertainment			
Transportation (Car Payments, Fuel, Bus)			
Clothing/Shoes			
School Expenses/Tuition			
Credit Card/Debt Payment			
Fees: Late, ATM, Money Order, Check Cashing			
Giving (Personal and Charity)			
Books, DVDs, and CDs			
Subscriptions/Dues (Magazines, Clubs)			
Insurance (Health, Car, Rental)			
Miscellaneous Daily Expenses			
Other:			
Other:			
TOTAL EXPENSES			
MONTHLY BALANCE TO SAVE (total income - total expenses)			

Housing Situation

Does this person rent or own? _____ Does this person have room-mates? ____yes ____no
Who do they live with? _____
Does this person have any dependents living with them? If so, who? _____
_____

Is it a temporary living situation? ____yes ____no
If yes, explain: _____
_____
_____

Is this person homeless? ____yes ____no
What type of housing does this person/family live in?
____Apt. ____House ____Room ____ Projects ____Section 8
____Shelter

Spiritual, Social, and Emotional/Mental Health

Describe the person's Christian experience/spiritual journey, if applicable:
_____
_____
_____

What sort of social supports does this person have? _____
_____

Does this individual have any family living nearby? ____yes ____no
If yes, who? _____
Any family members the person is close to? ____yes ____no
If yes, who? _____
_____

Does this individual have a church small group? ____yes ____no
If yes, name and phone number of leader: _____
_____

Do one or two close friends know of the person's situation?
____yes ____no

Is this person seeing a counselor? _____yes _____no

If yes, who? _____

Has this person ever been diagnosed and/or treated for a mental illness?

_____yes _____no

If yes, explain: _____

_____

_____

Is this person currently taking any prescribed medications?

_____yes _____no

Previous medications? _____yes _____no

If yes, what is/was the medication? _____

What condition is/was it for? _____

_____

Has the person ever been hospitalized for depression/suicide or other mental

illnesses? _____yes _____no

If yes, when and what for? _____

_____

_____

Has this person experienced trauma at some point in their life? If yes, de-

scribe:_____

_____

_____

SECTION 4: Church Assessment and Response to This Request

Remember that poverty has multiple causes: the individual's behavior, abusive or exploitive people, oppressive systems, and demonic forces. In many cases, more than one of these causes are at work. However, to the extent that the person's own behavior is a contributor, you should try to gauge their receptivity to taking actions to make positive changes in their life. In such cases, check the one that most applies:

This person/family believes:

1. _____There is no deep-seated problem that I/we need to address.

2. _____There may be a problem, but I'm/we aren't the one(s) who need to change.

3. _____ Yes, there is a problem, but I'm/we doubtful it can be changed.

4. _____ Yes, there is a problem, and I/we can be part of making needed changes, but is it worth it?

5. _____ Yes, there is a problem, and I/we are ready to take steps to make needed changes.

Category 1 or 2: This person/family is not ready to do the hard work of: (1) identifying areas that they need to change, and (2) making those changes with your church's help. They are not ready to create an action plan. Since you are using this form with people you believe need to begin the change process starting now, their lack of readiness to change might well disqualify them from receiving assistance from the church at this time. But that doesn't mean ignoring them. Through continued contact and conversation, they might develop more openness to change.

Categories 3–5: This person is ready to create an action plan.

- You may find that people in category 3 or 4 complete the action plan but then do not follow through on their goals. Do not give up! They will probably need extra encouragement and support, and their goals and timeframes may need to be adjusted. If they do not make sufficient progress on their goals even with repeated encouragement or help, then you and your church may need to stop providing the material and possible human resources that you committed to in the action plan. That does not mean you neglect the person/family or break your relationship with them! It just means you may have to shift the terms of the relationship.

- People in category 5 will have a bit smoother time of moving forward and contributing their part to their goal, although there will still be bumps, and thus need for support.

- Remember from chapter 2 that if the person has experienced trauma, progress may be slower or halting, with times of no progress and/or regression.

Initial church assessment of issues that need to be dealt with that contributed to current problem: _____

_____

_____

_____

_____

Initial response/decision: _____

_____

_____

_____

_____

SECTIONS 1 AND 2: IDENTIFYING INFORMATION AND CURRENT SITUATION

Section 1 of the intake form collects basic information about the person and how to contact them. It also records any current or past interactions with your church. Remember: based on your benevolence policies, current church involvement might factor in to whether or not you will provide financial assistance to the person.

This section also requests contact information for references to enable you to learn more about the person's story. Depending on the situation, you might choose not to ask for these references immediately. But if you move forward in assisting this person, be sure to collect this information, for you will want to contact these references to try to learn more about the person and their situation. Be aware that laws concerning confidentiality and privacy may prevent some of these references from being able to share information with you, especially if the reference is a physical or mental health professional.

Section 2 of the intake form records the particulars of the person's current situation and request. This is where you record the specific assistance the person is requesting such as, "I need help with my electric bill." *But remember: the person is usually only presenting the immediate, visible need.* This visible need is usually just the symptom of deeper, underlying problems. Many of the questions in the rest of the intake form are designed to help you to identify the circumstances or behaviors that have created this visible need, so you can move beyond treating the symptoms and get to the underlying disease.

As you listen to the person's story, prayerfully discern whether the situation basically requires relief or development. As you try to determine the appropriate response, you may find it helpful to ask yourself the following two questions:

1. Will a failure to provide immediate assistance likely result in serious harm?

If the answer to this question is clearly yes, you should provide relief, offering assistance to "stop the bleeding." For example, if a single mother and her three small children have been evicted from their apartment and it is 10 degrees outside, a failure to provide immediate assistance could result in real harm; you should provide relief to ensure that the family has adequate food and shelter.

However, your help might not stop there! A person needing immediate relief may also need development. If so, once relief has ended the crisis, you should seek to enter into a longer-term relationship with the person in which you work together to address the root causes of their poverty.

Note that when the person is in danger of *serious* harm, it does not matter whether or not their own behaviors caused the crisis. You must help them. Period.

But what if the answer to this question is no? What should you do if withholding assistance will not expose the person to serious harm but will simply allow their life to be a bit more unpleasant in the short run? The appropriate response in this more common situation is less clear and requires greater discernment. In such a situation, proceed to question 2.

2. Is the person largely responsible for their situation?

If the answer to this second question is truly no—e.g., the person was mugged or a tornado destroyed their home—you can usually provide immediate assistance without fear of fostering crippling dependency. You will not need to use sections 3 and 4 of the intake form in this situation.

One caveat to this is when the person is repeatedly experiencing the same crisis. You might still provide immediate assistance, but you may want to ask them to commit to working with you to find ways to prevent the crisis from happening repeatedly in the future. For example, if a person is repeatedly injured from slipping on the ice on their steps, you might work with them to ensure somebody clears the ice each morning.

The most difficult case is when the answer to question 2 is yes. For example, a person is short of money due to their refusal to work enough to pay their bills. The goal is not to punish people for their sins but to extend God's love. But what does love entail in this case?

Relief: Different Forms of Crisis

A couple in Nate's church were working hard, but still living month to month. Then their car unexpectedly died. The couple came to the church for help, and Nate looked over their finances. "I realized they were only eating one meal a day while trying to save for the car repair. I immediately calculated food costs for two months, and gave them that amount in gift cards to a grocery store." The couple managed to pay for the car repair, and they are still actively involved in the church. They have not needed financial assistance since.[4]

As you pray for wisdom to discern the best course of action, remember that truly loving the person is to seek to restore them to image-bearing: their being empowered to live in right relationship to God, self, others, and the rest of creation. As discussed in chapter 1, such empowerment means that people are growing in their ability to analyze their situation, make healthy decisions to improve the situation, and carry out those decisions in all four of these relationships. For example, part of living in right relationship to creation includes their ability to find and perform work that will enable them to support themselves and their families. Ask yourself in each situation: *Will providing immediate financial assistance help or hinder such empowerment?*

As discussed in chapter 1, allowing the person to experience some of the consequences of their actions can be the trigger needed for them to make necessary changes in their life. Thus, withholding *immediate and unconditional* financial assistance may be the best way to show love, *as long as doing so does not expose them to serious harm* (1 Timothy 5:3–13). You will still try to help this person, but the appropriate response will be development, not relief: any assistance—both immediate and future—will be conditional on their taking actions to contribute to their own improvement.

If you decide the person is in need of development rather than relief, ask the person if they are willing to engage in a longer-term process of change in order to get to the root causes of their problems. If the person seems willing, you can then use the rest of the intake form to further gauge their receptivity to change and to help the two of you—and their family—to determine what that change process might look like. Note that this longer-term process may or may not involve your providing them with material assistance, either now or in the future. But any such assistance will build upon their use of their own gifts, abilities, and resources in order to make positive changes in their life.

If the person indicates some willingness to address the core issues that are contributing to their poverty, you could proceed into completing some or all of section 3 on the intake form. But it is likely the person will need a break at this point. If so, you should request that they return for another meeting to complete section 3. Explain the documents and materials they will need to bring in order to complete this section.

Make sure to be sensitive and reassuring when asking the person to provide additional information, as this request could scare away some people who truly do want to work at improving their lives. Recall that a person who has experienced trauma could be especially guarded or suspicious. Try to assure the person that you need this information so your church can work with them on finding long-term solutions.

Some people will state they do not want to return to complete section 3 and that they just want immediate assistance. If the person is unwilling to return to meet with you to discuss the deeper factors contributing to their poverty—and if they do not need relief—you should typically decline their requests for immediate financial assistance. *This does not mean you are withholding all forms of assistance from them.* Rather, you are offering to help them by walking with them over time in a way that addresses the roots of their current situation. Whether or not they accept this help is outside of your control.

SECTION 3: DETAILED CONTEXT AND HISTORY

Some of the questions in section 3 might not be applicable or appropriate right away—as always, adapt as you go. It is a careful balance. On one hand, you do not want to scare people away by asking invasive questions before they have a trusting relationship with you. In particular, as discussed in chapter 2, you will need to be especially sensitive and patient when working with people who have experienced trauma. On the other hand, you *do* want to communicate that walking together is a longer-term, in-depth process and that you are not interested in just writing a check so they can continue in their current state. If the person requesting assistance is from your church, you will likely have an existing relationship and some context of trust. As a result, you can likely press further into these questions more quickly with them.

Questions about work history and educational level allow you to sense what someone's income potential might be, as well as what types of jobs they might be qualified to do.

The budgeting worksheet allows both of you to see where an individual's resources—whether in the form of wages, food stamps, Social Security, or other assistance—are being spent. Focus first on completing the sections in the second column entitled "current income" and "current expenses." Over time, you can fill out the remaining columns by exploring with them any changes they can make to their income or expenses in order to create a new budget that will enable them to live within their means.

As you examine these issues together, you will often have an opportunity to delve into the deeper issues of the person's life, which is where many of the core causes of their poverty can be found. By gently asking the right questions, it is possible to initiate many triggers for change:

- *Do you see any large expenditures that surprise you?*
- *Why do you think you spend so much money on this item? What role does this item play in your life?*
- *You said that you smoke cigarettes to deal with anxiety. What are the reasons for anxiety in your life? Are there other ways to reduce this anxiety?*
- *What prevents you from increasing your income?*

Going deeper is a process; it cannot all be done in one sitting. Use the budget as a forum for ongoing discussions, looking for ways to help people to become more empowered to live in right relationship with God, self, others, and the rest of creation. And as you walk with them in this way, be open to what God might want to teach you about your own finances and what your income and expenditures reveal about the deeper issues in your own life. It isn't just low-income people who need to be more empowered!

Of course, putting a new budget on paper is not the same as living it out. Adjusting income or expenditure patterns usually involves making painful lifestyle changes that require both encouragement and accountability. As will be discussed further below, it is crucial that your benevolence ministry have an individual or team who will be able to walk with this person over time, providing them with the support they will need.

Additional resources can provide you with the process of budgeting, financial education, going deeper, and supporting people over time. In particular, chapter 5 describes *Faith & Finances*, a set of resources that many churches and ministries are using to foster learning communities that empower people to better steward their finances.

The other questions in section 3 are designed to gain a sense of an individual's support systems, family life, spiritual status, emotional health, and experience with trauma. Again, you will need to be sensitive about asking these questions. Prayerfully feel your way through the conversation, looking for the best time to explore these issues more deeply. Not everything needs to be done in one sitting . . . it's a process!

Look for patterns: Does this person lack a supportive community? Has this person previously had supportive networks but alienated them? Are there other complicating factors, such as mental illness or other medical needs? Is there any evidence that this person is experiencing ongoing abuse? Remember: poverty is complex and can result from a combination of individual behaviors, abusive or exploitive people, oppressive systems, or demonic forces. The questions on this intake form can give you an initial glimpse into how these complex factors are manifesting themselves in this individual's life.

SECTION 4: CHURCH ASSESSMENT AND RESPONSE TO THIS REQUEST

At the end of section 2, you paused to do an early assessment of whether or not the person seemed willing to address the deeper factors contributing to their poverty. Your conversations with the person as you complete section 3 should now enable you to gauge the person's receptivity to change more fully. Use section 4 to write down your *tentative* conclusions.

Again, do not write anyone off too quickly. Some people might be tired of their lifestyle and chronic poverty, and as you talk with them, they may recognize that they need to change. But it might take time for them to believe that those changes are possible. It might also take time for them to trust your offer to join hands with them to tackle the obstacles that they face. Prioritize kindness, patience, and grace as you assess their willingness to change. And be open to the possibility that your initial conclusions could be wrong. The person who walks away from you today might be back in a week, sincerely ready and willing to change.

CHECKING THE FACTS ON THE INTAKE FORM

One of the purposes of completing an intake form is to provide you with concrete information about a person. As discussed in chapter 3, you then have the opportunity—within the bounds of federal and state privacy laws—to fact-check the person's story by contacting references, other churches or agencies that have helped them, or any community databases.

The point of this fact-checking process is not solely to determine if the person is being truthful with you in order to decide whether or not to give them assistance. Rather, you should see it as an opportunity to get a more complete picture of this person and the situation in order to be able to help more effectively. And if your fact-checking reveals that the story the person told you is not completely true, it provides you with yet another opportunity to go deeper with this person, asking reflective questions that can trigger long-term, positive change:

- *Why do you think you misreported this information?*
- *Are there other areas in your life where you are being less than truthful with others or with yourself?*
- *How can we develop a trusting relationship with one another if we are not being completely truthful?*

USING AN ACTION PLAN

If the person's words and behaviors indicate willingness to address the underlying factors contributing to their poverty, you can begin the difficult but rewarding experience of walking with them through the development process.

The single most important tool for beginning this long-term process is an action plan, which is an intentional mechanism to help people to be empowered to live in right relationship with God, self, others, and the rest of creation. In an action plan, the person commits to taking specific steps in order to achieve their own goals, and your church agrees to provide appropriate support, encouragement, and accountability to complement the person's efforts.

You can complete an action plan with the person in a single meeting or over the course of several meetings. As discussed in chapter 2, when dealing with a person who has experienced trauma, it will be particularly important that you do not go too fast, as the person may feel threatened by a sense of vulnerability or a loss of control at the thought of being accountable to people who they might not even know.

Below is an example action plan consistent with the asset-based, participatory approach described in chapter 1, followed by further explanation and guidance for each of the sections. We have adapted and expanded it with permission from Diaconal Ministries Canada.

TOOL 3—ACTION PLAN[5]

WORKING TOGETHER FOR GROWTH AND CHANGE

SECTION 1: Reflection

A. Where You Want to Be: How would you like your life situation to be different or improved four to six months from now?

Goal 1:_____

Goal 2:_____

Optional Questions:

- Do you think those goals are consistent with God's desire for your life?
- Where do you think He would like you to be in four to six months?
- Would you like to make any revisions to your goals?

B. Abilities and Resources:

What are some abilities and resources you have that could help you get to where you want to be four to six months from now? _____

_____

_____

_____

C. Obstacles:

It is good to be aware of things that might get in the way of you getting to where you want to be four to six months from now. It can be helpful to specifically list possible key obstacles. Doing so can help all of us be aware of them and create plans to overcome them or at least lessen their impact.

Internal obstacles (things about your personality or habits that could block or slow progress): _____

_____

_____

_____

External obstacles (people or situations that could block or slow progress):

_____

_____

_____

_____

SECTION 2: Planning for the Future Together

A. Things You Want to Do: Steps that will move you to where you want to be in four to six months:

Goal 1 _____

What specific things can you do?	Do this by when?
(a) _____	_____
(b) _____	_____
(c) _____	_____

Goal 2 _____

What specific things can you do?	Do this by when?
(a) _____	_____
(b) _____	_____
(c) _____	_____

B. Things We Can Do to Support You: How can church members help you get to where you want to be in four to six months?

Goal 1 (from above)_____

What specific things can the church do?	Do this by when?
(a) _____	_____
(b) _____	_____
(c) _____	_____

Goal 2 (from above)_____

What specific things can the church do?	Do this by when?
(a) _____	_____
(b) _____	_____
(c) _____	_____

SECTION 3: Encouragement and Accountability
A. Supportive People:[6]

It is hard for most of us to make changes alone. Therefore, as part of helping you toward your goals, we have an individual/team who would like to support you through prayers and encouragement. They have promised to:

- Pray for you every day.
- Talk with you at least once a week. This will be to see how you are doing and give you input as you desire.
- Keep information confidential as is appropriate.

Would you be willing to have an individual/team support you in your goals?_____
Name of supportive individual/team leader: _____
Phone: _____

B. Follow-up:

Plans fail if they get lost in the hectic nature of life, so staying in communication with each other is very important. It will help all involved to see how things are progressing and how the plan might need to be adjusted to reach your goals. Normally communication will be more frequent in the beginning of implementing the action plan to ensure that momentum is gained.

When and how or where can we next get together to check how things are going? _____
_____
_____
Other conditions of agreement: _____
_____
_____
Signature of individual: _____
_____
    Date _____
Signature of church representative:_____
    Date _____

SECTION 1: REFLECTION

The first section of the action plan provides a context for the person to reflect on his or her own life. As you work on this section together, be careful not to do the reflection *for* them, crowding out their thoughts and ideas with your own. Let them think. Let them speak. Remember: they must own the process and be in the driver's seat in order to do the hard work of pursuing change. At the same time, it may be difficult for some people to dream and to express hope, so you might need to prompt and encourage them a bit to consider new possibilities for their life.

You will notice that the first question asks people to dream about what they would like their lives to look like in four to six months—not five or ten years. Most of the time, change comes in frustratingly small steps. Remember the principle discussed at the end of chapter 3: one of the keys to unleashing change is to *start small, start fast,* and *succeed.*[7] Encourage the individual to dream about *small, concrete,* and *obtainable* ways that their lives could be different in the near future. For example, the goals could be:

- I will try to pay my rent on time two months in a row.
- I will reduce my food expenditures by $50 per month over the next three months.
- I will enroll in a course at the local community college.

The optional questions in section 1. A (Where You Want to Be) require some explanation. It is important that people set their own goals so they will own them. For this reason, the action plan starts by asking the person what *they* want *their* life to look like in four to six months, and the rest of the form focuses on what *they* will do to achieve *their* goals and how you can help them in this process. Although this approach does help people to own their process of change, it has the potential downside of encouraging them to be self-centered, as the focus is all on them and their desires. But the primary question that all of us need to be asking is not: What do I want for my life? Rather, we need to be asking: What does God want for my life? How can I use my life to glorify Him?

In this light, if you know that the individual is a Christian or is at least open to Christian concepts, it might be good to use the optional questions in section 1. A in order to redirect the person away from themselves and to point them to God. However, if you do not believe that the person is open to this sort of discussion, you can skip the optional questions for the moment. As your relationship with this person unfolds, you can then look for opportunities to point them toward a more God-centered life.

An Empowering Process

"My end goal is to be able to 'hand the pen' to this person so they can author their own story . . . seeing beyond the need that is being presented, asking, 'What is really preventing them from being able to write their own story?'"

—**NATE,** STAFF MEMBER AT GRACE FELLOWSHIP CHURCH[8]

After section 1. A, the plan focuses on identifying the abilities and resources the person can use to achieve their stated goals. In addition to thinking about their own gifts, encourage them to reflect on the friendships, family members, and other networks that could support them in making changes in their lives. Most people need ongoing encouragement and accountability to repeatedly go through the change cycle described in chapter 1.

When identifying obstacles to change, start with those that are internal, such as particular bents, habits, or choices. For example, the habit of spending money impulsively on nonnecessities rather than paying off bills, reducing debt, or saving would be an internal obstacle. When discussing these internal obstacles, it is often helpful to be open and transparent about your own bad habits and struggles in order to help the person feel more comfortable. In addition, this posture provides another chance to communicate and apply the good news of the gospel: we are all broken, but Jesus Christ can and does make all things new, including us!

The external obstacles to change could include anything from an abusive spouse to a more macro-level issue as a shortage of jobs in your community. Discuss which external obstacles can be addressed in the foreseeable future. For those external obstacles that cannot be remedied soon, try to determine how to minimize the damage they are causing. In addition, your benevolence ministry should communicate these "immovable obstacles" to the larger church body as a possible issue to be addressed over the long haul. For example, if employment opportunities are slim, perhaps your church could recruit business owners to offer more jobs to low-income people in your community.

SECTION 2: PLANNING FOR THE FUTURE TOGETHER

In setting goals and determining concrete action steps, your role is to keep people realistic about what can be accomplished and create a series of highly attainable steps to getting there. Again: *start small, start fast,* and *succeed.* The disappointment of failing to reach a goal has the potential to derail the change process. In this light, it is important to recognize that because each person is unique, the number of goals and action steps will necessarily vary from person to person. You have to adjust to the unique personality, capacity, and pace of the particular individual with whom you are working.

The next set of questions in the action plan is focused on your church. Take the goals and action steps the individual created and ask, "How can we help you to accomplish these goals?" Again, create specific and realistic commitments. Trust is absolutely essential for this process to work well over time, and trust can be deeply broken if your church does not follow through on its commitments.

SECTION 3: SUPPORT, ENCOURAGEMENT, AND ACCOUNTABILITY

One of the primary tasks in church benevolence work is recruiting and equipping people from your congregation to walk alongside low-income individuals and families as they pursue the change process, which will be discussed in chapter 5. The above form suggests some potential roles for these volunteers, but you can revise the list of responsibilities in light of the capacities of your benevolence workers and volunteers from your church.

You will need to ask the person you are helping if they would be comfortable having an individual or team from the congregation support them in the change process. This may be an idea that needs to be introduced over time as the person grows in their trust of your church and its ministry, particularly if the person has experienced trauma.

No plan is worth anything unless it is followed, so determine how often you will touch base and when your next follow-up meeting will be. Although it is crucial to meet face-to-face regularly, it is also possible to touch base through phone calls, emails, or texts. Discuss the means of communicating that will be easiest and most effective for the individual.

One factor to consider when determining your follow-up schedule is where you are going to meet. Sooner rather than later, be sure that one of those meetings is in the person's home. Part of the trust involved in a deepening relationship involves entering the person's world and embracing them in it. In addition, going into their home allows them to give back by hosting you. If the person is not open to your being in their home, you might want to gently try to determine the reason. Sometimes family situations or living conditions are embarrassing to people. But if you can enter into their world—accepting them "warts and all"—it can be a powerful way of communicating the warmth of our heavenly Father's deep embrace.

One word of caution: do not visit the person's home alone. Take at least one other person with you in order to avoid the appearance of a compromising situation, and reduce the exposure of the church member to any harm.

One of the greatest tools in encouraging people to follow through in the change process is simply to remind them of their action steps. For many people, life is busy and things get overlooked. And as discussed in chapter 2, avoidance behavior can be a deeply ingrained pattern of behavior for people who have experienced trauma. Regardless of the reason, a quick text message or phone call can be very helpful: "Remember we're going to meet next Tuesday, and you're going to have all your receipts from this week with you!" Of course, if you remind the person over and over again and get no response, you will need to determine if the person just views your reminders as nagging.

The close of the action plan includes space to record any other conditions unique to the individual situation, as well as a space for the person and a representative of your church to sign. Before signing the document, it would be wise to give both the person and the member of your benevolence team time to think and pray through the commitments being proposed. It is much better for both parties to sincerely own these commitments than to find out that they really were not ready or fully on board.

The person seeking help may very well be frustrated by the slowness of the process. After all, their initial hope was probably that you would quickly write them a check to help them to deal with their immediate need. While you do not want to discourage the person, do not feel rushed to start giving money to them, unless there is real danger of harm. Especially do not let their sense of urgency—"The power company is going to turn off my electricity in two days!"—cause you to give out money too early in the change process.

Note that their completing the action plan does not mean that you should now immediately give them money! As discussed in chapter 1, because we North Americans tend to believe poverty is largely about a lack of material things, we often provide money too soon and in too large a quantity. Remember, the process of development is one of bringing in outside resources—financial, human, and technical—in ways that build on the person's use of their own gifts, abilities, and resources.

For example, if the person's action plan is to enroll in the local community college, you might agree to pay a portion of the tuition directly to the school as long as the individual makes satisfactory progress in the program.

And if the action plan is focused on no longer being in debt to the electric company, you could go to the electric company together to set up a plan to pay off the debt that has been accumulated. You can then work with the person to design a plan to pay off this debt and to avoid falling into debt again. Part of this plan could include your agreeing to pay off one dollar of the person's debt for every two dollars of debt they pay off themselves. You should make your payments directly to the electric company after you receive balance statements proving that the individual has made their own debt reduction payments.

It is generally good practice that the person pay for at least 50 percent of the initiative in the action plan, e.g., at least 50 percent of the tuition to attend the local community college or at least 50 percent of the debt reduction with the electric company. However, each situation is different, and there is no absolute rule. You will need to ask God to give you wisdom about the best way to proceed in each case.

Development-Style Assistance

Nate shares a story of what material assistance can look like in the development process. Mike, a military veteran in his congregation who struggled with mental illness, approached the church for help. He was living in transitional housing and struggling to cover his financial needs. Mike had assistance from Veteran's Affairs on the way and had filed for disability, but he was waiting for the paperwork to go through.

Nate's church worked to connect him to different housing, and helped cover some of his utilities and transportation costs in the meantime. "We saw him twice a week, and he helped tear down after church and Bible studies. I had no problem helping him, because he was on a trajectory of trying to become more stable and was actively involved in our church."

There have certainly been bumps in the road. At one point, Mike disappeared for several weeks, skipping meetings with his ally. However, Mike eventually reached out again. The church has persevered, continuing to walk alongside him through the ups and downs of the development process.[9]

Note how different these examples are from the common dynamic: "Okay, I have completed your action plan. Can you now give me the money I asked for so that I can pay my electric bill?" Do not give away money too early or too often, for doing so can undermine the longer-term process of change that is embodied in the action plan.

Once both parties have signed the action plan, you now have a concrete agreement that serves as a foundation for embarking on the process of change together. Be sure to finish your time together by praying over the plan. Ask God to move in this situation and ask Him to mold all of you in this undertaking.

BEYOND THE ACTION PLAN

Throughout the course of the follow-up meetings, the action plan will inevitably need updates and revisions. Timelines might need to be readjusted or steps reordered. If the goals in the action plan are achieved, make sure to celebrate! Recognize and mark the accomplishment. Take the person out to lunch or give a gift card to a grocery store. They have accomplished something! Make sure you applaud their progress. Then it might be time to create another action plan that moves the individual or family further along the path of development.

For example, it can take several months to accurately track revenues and expenses, particularly if they fluctuate quite a bit. Thus, someone's first action plan might be focused on simply tracking revenues and expenses and on working with you to create a realistic budget. The next action plan might focus on following the budget, creating an emergency fund, and beginning to pay off small debts. The action plan process should be repeated over and over as you walk with the individual across time.

Working with people in this developmental way is much more difficult than simply giving them money to pay their electric bill. It is time-consuming and requires intense work. *You cannot do this all on your own.* You must access these three additional resources in order to be able to sustain the change process:

1. Volunteers to provide ongoing support, encouragement, and accountability;
2. Other ministries and services available in your community;
3. Existing or new ministries in your church.

The next chapter explores how to access or develop these resources in order to make your benevolence ministry both more powerful and sustainable.

TASK TO COMPLETE: Adopt an Intake Form and Action Plan

Create an intake form and action plan for your benevolence ministry. If you already have these forms, consider any revisions that you might like to make in light of the content of this chapter. If you do not have these forms yet, you can adapt the examples provided in this chapter for your own ministry and context.

EXPLORE ONLINE RESOURCES

Create an account on the Chalmers Center's User Portal to access some of the tools and resources mentioned in this chapter.

Create an Account At:
www.helpingwithouthurting.org/benevolence

Enter Access Code: walkwith

CHAPTER 5

AMBASSADORS OF RECONCILIATION

BUILDING YOUR CHURCH'S CAPACITY FOR BENEVOLENCE WORK

As we have seen, walking with people developmentally often requires significant time and human resources.

Your benevolence team cannot do all of this on its own, so you will need to identify and mobilize additional help. This might sound like hard work, and it is. But don't view it in purely negative terms, for as you engage others in the process of reconciling relationships, you are enabling them to live out their identity as a "new creation" in Christ as well:

> Therefore, if anyone is in Christ, the new creation has come: the old
> has gone, the new is here! All this is from God, who reconciled us to
> himself through Christ and gave us the ministry of reconciliation:
> that God was reconciling the world to himself in Christ, not counting
> people's sins against them. And he has committed to us the message of
> reconciliation. (2 Corinthians 5:17–19)

Christians are a new creation in Christ, who are called to bring His reconciliation to bear on a hurting world. And there is no better place to start than with the Bens and Debbies who are walking through the front doors of your church.

In this light, one of the key skills needed in a benevolence team is the ability to identify and mobilize other individuals and ministries to be involved in this reconciling work. This skill includes recruiting individuals, delegating tasks to them, and identifying and accessing the services of other ministries or organizations. This chapter discusses this important skill, focusing on three primary resources you should use to strengthen and sustain your benevolence ministry:

1. Volunteers to provide ongoing support, encouragement, and accountability
2. Other ministries and services available in your community
3. Existing or new ministries in your church

RECRUITING AND EQUIPPING VOLUNTEERS

As discussed in chapter 4, supportive individuals or teams from your church are vital for providing low-income people with encouragement and accountability as they seek to complete their action plans. Unfortunately, it is usually much easier to find people willing to donate money to your ministry than it is to find people who are willing to invest the time and energy needed to walk with people in longer-term relationships. Of course, your benevolence ministry does need money, but the scarcest resource is people who are willing to walk with low-income people over time.

In this light, it is extremely important that the pastor and other church leaders are regularly discipling the congregation to understand both the biblical mandate to care for the poor as well as the relational nature of poverty. The congregation needs to understand that—in addition to giving their money—they must "spend" themselves on behalf of the hungry and oppressed (Isaiah 58:10). Yes, low-income people need our financial resources, but even more they need relationships with us . . . and we need relationships with them. You need to recruit volunteers, and the most effective recruitment tool is the Holy Spirit impressing the Word of God into the hearts of the members of your congregation.

And as this happens, you should make it easy for people to volunteer for your benevolence ministry through blurbs in your church bulletin, postings on the church's website and Facebook page, announcements during services, and flyers displayed around the church. In addition, nothing is as effective as a personal invitation to people you know well in the church: "Jake, I've been watching you, and I think God has given you the gift of encouragement. Would you be willing . . ."

Of course, not everybody who volunteers for the task of walking with low-income people in a longer-term relationship is qualified for the task. Indeed, as discussed in chapter 1, relationships between the materially poor and non-poor often do considerable harm, particularly when the materially non-poor have a sense of superiority. Thus, the most important quality to look for in volunteers is evidence that they deeply understand and live out the good news of the gospel: *We were all profoundly broken people who deserved eternal punishment; but through Christ's death and resurrection—and absolutely no merit of our own—we are now the adopted sons and daughters of our heavenly Father* (Galatians 4:1–7). You will want to informally screen volunteers to make sure they fit this profile.

More than Recruitment

"We believe we need those who come from different backgrounds to speak into our lives. We challenge members of our congregation to not see themselves as the helpers."

—NATE, STAFF MEMBER AT GRACE FELLOWSHIP CHURCH[1]

Here are a few more tips to guide you in the recruitment process:

• Do not call these volunteers "mentors" to the low-income people. This language establishes the superior-inferior, fixer-fixed dynamic described in chapter 1, rather than a healthy relationship centered on mutual growth. Some ministries refer to these volunteer encouragers as "allies" or "champions."

- Be clear about the time commitment you are asking of the volunteers, both in terms of the overall length of time as well as the expectations within that timeframe. For example, you might say: "This opportunity is a six-month commitment, which will entail two to three contacts per week for the first two months then one or two contacts per week for the following four months. Contacts could include any of the following: a meeting of one to two hours to encourage the person and to help them solve problems as they seek to follow their action plans; a phone call of fifteen to thirty minutes in which you pray with them; or a text message telling them you are thinking of them and encouraging them to carry out the tasks outlined in their action plan. Of course, you may spend more time if you desire, but that isn't required or expected." Do not use language that makes it sound like you are asking the volunteers to befriend this person in an unlimited and unending way. While new, long-term friendships may arise out of this situation, you are not asking the volunteers to commit to such an open-ended relationship.

- Be clear about the training they will need to go through before they begin serving as a volunteer. More about this training will be discussed below.

- Be clear about what the task is and is not. The task is about giving encouragement, problem solving *with* the person not *for* them, providing accountability to complete the action plan, praying together for each other, and connecting the person with additional help as is appropriate. The task is not about the volunteer providing money or other material assistance.

- Some churches use a team-based approach, which can be very helpful for both the low-income person and the volunteers. In this approach, one or two people focus on the interpersonal relationship with the low-income person, while the others on the team are willing to babysit, provide rides, help with other tasks, and so on.

Be sure it is clear to everyone on the team that the low-income person must lead the process of changing his or her own life and that the team is simply there as support in this process. For more information on using a team-based approach, see *Establishing a Church-Based Welfare-to-Work Mentoring Ministry: A Practical "How-To" Manual* by Dr. Amy L. Sherman, which is available online by following the directions at the end of this chapter.

• Let volunteers know that the benevolence team will back them up and step in as needed. They are not alone in this process.

• After you have clarified all the expectations, you should have the volunteer sign a simple statement agreeing to the terms and guidelines of the commitment.

• Be sure to do more than just say "thank you" to the volunteer after the commitment has been fulfilled. Provide a small token of thanks such as a small gift card, a volunteer recognition ceremony, or a special dinner.

You will want to provide some basic training to prepare your volunteers for this exciting but challenging work. It is imperative they understand the core concepts of chapter 1 of this book, including:

• Poverty is fundamentally rooted in broken relationships due to individual behaviors, abusive or exploitive people, oppressive systems, and demonic forces. As a result, it cannot be easily solved through handouts of material resources.

• Poverty alleviation is about reconciling relationships, a process that includes walking *with* people in empowering ways across time, not doing things *to* or *for* people.

• Poverty alleviation is not primarily about getting a current problem solved—e.g., paying an electric bill—or even about meeting a certain goal such as getting a college degree. It is fundamentally about people being restored to image-bearing: being empowered to live in right relationship to God, self, others, and the rest of creation. Such empowerment means that people are growing in their ability to analyze their situation, to make healthy decisions to improve their situation, and to carry out those decisions in all four of these relationships. *This is the goal; getting the electric bill paid off quickly is not the goal!*

- In order to achieve this goal, we should use an asset-based, participatory approach.

- Fundamentally, poverty cannot be solved without the transforming power of Jesus Christ and the indwelling of the Holy Spirit.

Some resources you will find helpful in communicating these core concepts include:

- Chapter 1 of this book

- *When Helping Hurts: How to Alleviate Poverty without Hurting the Poor . . . and Yourself* by Steve Corbett and Brian Fikkert

- *When Helping Hurts: The Small Group Experience* by Steve Corbett and Brian Fikkert. This study guide and online videos communicate the core concepts in a highly accessible way. Visit www.chalmers .org/small-group to learn more.

- Chalmers' *Helping without Hurting Seminar*: The four hours of video content summarizes the ideas in *When Helping Hurts* and prepares your leadership team or church to engage in effective poverty alleviation. Visit www.chalmers.org/hwh-seminar to learn more.

In addition, *Equipping Allies* applies these core concepts to the actual practice of being an "ally" to a low-income person. Further information is available online by following the directions at the end of this chapter.

We have just described a simple pathway to get you moving with respect to recruiting and equipping volunteers. But you can also use a more comprehensive approach—an *asset-mapping exercise*—to mobilize your congregation on a larger scale. An asset-mapping exercise can move people toward being more engaged in poverty alleviation in general and in your benevolence ministry in particular. Through an asset-mapping exercise, you can create a more detailed picture of:

- The gifts and resources in your church
- The needs your congregation is best positioned to address
- The types of ministries your church might consider establishing
- The types of needs that your church cannot address
- The people who might be the best fit for various volunteer or staff positions

For example, you might discover that you have a significant number of people in your church who are passionate about and gifted in caring for children. They might be willing to provide classes or day care while your benevolence team meets with their parents; or perhaps they might be interested in starting an after-school program that ministers to kids while their parents are at work.

You might also discover people in your church who are available to provide transportation during the week, driving an individual to a job interview, a doctor's appointment, or a court hearing, for example.

Other people might be excellent advocates in your community, using their connections and networks to address community-level issues in the educational, judicial, or financial systems.

Similarly, some members might be well connected in the business community and could link low-income people to potential employers.

Finally, you might also see how the church facilities can be a more useful kingdom resource for low-income people.

Ultimately, mapping the assets of your church is a way of helping both individuals and the congregation as a whole to see the gifts that God has given them in light of the needs of the low-income people in your community. While asset mapping is not an essential step to building your benevolence ministry, it is often an energizing process, providing people with enthusiasm and motivation to use their gifts to advance your church's ministry.

The tool titled *Church Asset-Mapping* can be used to conduct this exercise. Again, it is available for download by following the instructions at the end of the chapter.

> ### TASKS TO COMPLETE: Recruit and Equip Volunteers
> • Talk to your pastor and church leaders, asking them to increase their discipleship of the congregation with respect to poverty.
> • Determine if you will use individuals or teams of allies to provide encouragement and accountability. You should read Establishing a Church-Based Welfare-to-Work Mentoring Ministry: A Practical "How-To" Manual by Dr. Amy L. Sherman, to help you with this decision.
> • Prepare a document that clearly states the expectations of the volunteers; you will ask volunteers to sign this document in order to commit to being an ally for an individual or family as they seek to complete their action plan.
> • Decide which materials you will use to train volunteers, and how and when you will offer this training.
> • Get the word out in your church about volunteer opportunities with your benevolence team; decide if you will use the asset-mapping exercise as part of this process, either now or in the future.

CREATING A RESOURCE DIRECTORY OF MINISTRIES AND SERVICES IN YOUR COMMUNITY

In addition to mobilizing volunteers and other resources from your congregation, it is important for your church to know what other ministries and services are available in your community. Sometimes a low-income person will face challenges or needs that are beyond the scope of what your church can realistically and effectively address. In these scenarios, connecting them to another ministry or resource that can address those challenges can be a powerful way of strengthening your benevolence work.

Your search for resources should include churches and Christian organizations that are seeking to be "ambassadors of reconciliation," as well as services provided by nonsectarian organizations and government agencies. The Community Resource Directory you create should include each organization or ministry's name, address, telephone number, email, website, and a contact person, if available. You should also include information about the services they offer and their basic policies, fees, and hours of service.

In metropolitan areas, a good place to start searching for this type of information is the United Way, which often has a master list of services online. In addition, public social service agencies will also typically have some sort of directory. There may not be a listing of Christian ministries in your area, so you will often need to ask churches and Christian organizations you know of about any other ministries in the area. And do not forget to ask the low-income people you encounter, for they are often very knowledgeable of the existing services in the community.

Start by compiling information on the core ministries and organizations whose services you will most frequently want to access, and then expand the directory over time. Creating this directory might be a great task for a small group, Sunday school class, summer intern, or a high school or college group.

The tool below lists some of the types of resources you should consider including in your directory. Select from or add to this list in order to best fit your church's context and ministry. For your convenience, you can again download this tool by following the instructions at the end of the chapter.

TOOL 4—CREATING A COMMUNITY RESOURCE DIRECTORY[2]

GENERAL ASSISTANCE
- Local Social Services Department
  - Temporary Aid for Needy Families
  - Supplemental Security Income
  - Medicaid
  - Utility Assistance
- Food/Clothing/Furniture Closets or Pantries

HOUSING
- Emergency Shelters
- Domestic Abuse Shelters
- Rental Assistance Programs
- Federally Subsidized Housing Locations
- Mortgage Assistance Programs
- New Homeowners Assistance

CONSUMER INFORMATION
- Financial Literacy Programs
- Consumer Credit Counseling Service
- Volunteers in Tax Assistance (VITA)

EMPLOYMENT/VOCATIONAL
- Jobs Preparedness Programs
- Occupational Work Centers

EDUCATION
- Literacy Programs
- Tutoring Programs
- Graduate Equivalence Degree Programs
- College/Vocational Schools

HEALTH
- Crisis Pregnancy Centers
- Addiction Recovery Programs
- Public Health Clinics
- Public Health Nurses
- Parish Nurses
- Health-Care Social Workers
- Public Health Information Hotlines and Programs
- Trauma-Informed Care Centers

LEGAL
- Legal Aid Services
- Immigration Services
- Lawyers

- Magistrates and Other Court Officers
- Juvenile Justice Office

AGING PROGRAMS
- Subsidized Housing for Seniors
- Nutrition Centers for Seniors
- Developmental Day-Care Centers for Seniors
- Local Government's Office of Aging
- Nursing Homes

CHILDREN/YOUTH
- Head Start Programs
- Child Development Centers
- Infant Nutrition Centers
- Child Abuse/Neglect Social Workers
- Day Care and Nursery Schools
- Mentoring Programs (e.g., Big Brother/Sister)
- School Guidance Counselors
- After-School Tutoring Programs

HANDICAPPED SERVICES
- Rehabilitation Centers
- Developmental Activity Centers
- Numerous Special Interest Organizations

TASKS TO COMPLETE: Create a Community Resource Directory

- *Using Tool 4, pick five to ten categories of resources you want to find information about.*

- *Locate directories of ministries and services available for your town, city, or county.*

- *Plan how you will complete the first version of your Community Resource Directory.*

UTILIZING EXISTING OR NEW MINISTRIES IN YOUR CHURCH

A third resource for you to use are your church's own ministries, both the existing ones and any new ones that could be started.

Start by looking at the ministries that already exist. Do they address needs that are common among the low-income people your benevolence team encounters? Could they be modified to better serve your benevolence ministry? Are there any ways to better link this ministry to your benevolence work?

As you consider your church's existing ministries, do not overlook the power of your church's "ordinary" ministry—the preaching of the Word, baptism and the Lord's Supper, accountability and discipline, prayer. As described in chapter 1, these routine activities—offered in the context of a nurturing church family—are the very means that God has ordained to draw people into a saving relationship with Jesus Christ and to be nurtured in that relationship. You might want to discuss the following questions with your church's leadership:

- Is the "ordinary" ministry of your church accessible—culturally, socially, economically, and intellectually—to the people with whom the benevolence ministry is walking?
- What specific changes could your church make so this "ordinary" ministry is more accessible?
- Would a low-income person feel comfortable in your church family and be able to fully participate?
- What specific changes could your church make so low-income people could feel like members of your church family?

In addition, as you go through the process of identifying the existing resources in your community and church, you might see a gap your church could uniquely address. If so, your church could consider introducing a new ministry to help bring lasting change to the low-income individuals and households you are encountering.

While these gaps could be due to an important service simply not existing at all, they could also be due to the service being inadequate for accomplishing the objectives of the gospel-centered, developmental approach described in this book. Although your church should outsource to existing organizations any tasks in which you do not bring any distinct value added, do not use secular organizations to provide services in which your church has a unique opportunity to develop intentional relationships, share the gospel, and disciple people in a biblical worldview.

The Church: The Soil for Transformation

When Cody first started attending Nate's church, he had spent half his adult life in prison and was living transitionally in a shelter. Cody slowly began getting plugged into the church and asked Nate for financial help to launch a community outreach he was planning in his neighborhood. "We told him we couldn't provide money upfront in that way, but that I had a different idea about how we could work together when he was ready to talk about it," Nate recounts. Cody wrestled with the church's response, and actually considered leaving the church. But he eventually approached Nate about his idea.

Nate invited Cody to his church's *Faith & Finances* class, a ministry platform the church had started to walk alongside people who approached the church for assistance. In these classes, Cody developed relationships with people in the church, learned money management skills, and explored how his money could be part of God's work in the world. He graduated from the class and began saving his money in a bank account in which Nate's church matched the money Cody saved.

Cody has now purchased a pickup truck and uses it for ministry and outreach in his neighborhood. Further, Nate shares, "He has now been part of our church for three or four years, and just became a deacon at our church. He came to us from a shelter and is now in our leadership structure." By enfolding Cody in the church community, and by offering practical and biblically based training opportunities, both Grace Fellowship and Cody have experienced deep transformation.[3]

For example, if you are trying to help people to manage their finances more effectively, you might want to help them to open up a savings account and provide them with financial education. Which of these tasks should you outsource to other service providers, and which of these tasks should your church provide?

If banks in your community can provide savings accounts to low-income people, it would be silly for your church to start a bank. Existing banks provide savings accounts better than your church could, so you should just use their banking services!

In contrast, even if financial education courses are already being offered in your community, your church should still consider starting a ministry to provide this type of training. In particular, if the existing financial education programs are not teaching money management from a biblical perspective, they will fail to address the underlying heart and worldview issues that are often at the root of material poverty. Addressing these issues is the very thing that the church of Jesus Christ is uniquely positioned to do. *Again, do not outsource to secular service providers those features of the development process in which your church has a unique opportunity to develop intentional relationships, share the gospel, and disciple people in a biblical worldview.*

Of course, before you start a new ministry, make sure no other church or Christian organization is already offering this ministry in a gospel-centered, developmental way, lest you reinvent the wheel. If such a ministry does exist, you should consider connecting your benevolence ministry to it and supporting it with your human, financial, and spiritual resources. For example, if another church is already offering biblically based financial education, you could support it with trainers, allies, and money. Unfortunately, churches often struggle to cooperate with other churches or with existing ministries. Although there can be legitimate reasons not to collaborate, too often pride and competitiveness are the root causes for failing to work together. We must repent of these attitudes, for collaboration is good stewardship of kingdom resources, is part of our testimony to the world, and is pleasing to our Lord (John 17:20–23). This is another reason that it is so important to create the Community Resource Directory mentioned earlier.

While every church and community is different, resources to complement your benevolence work are described below. You can learn more about them online by following the directions at the end of this chapter.

1. *Financial Education Ministry* helps low-income people with budgeting, paying off debt, saving for the future, navigating the financial system, and making painful lifestyle changes to get their finances in order. When Ben asks for help with his rent or Debbie seeks assistance in paying her electric bill, having a financial education ministry in place can greatly strengthen your benevolence ministry. One option for you to consider is the Chalmers Center's *Faith & Finances* program, a set of biblically based financial education resources that churches and ministries are using to foster an empowering community in which the materially poor and materially non-poor learn and grow together.

2. *Jobs Preparedness Ministry* helps low-income people develop the soft skills necessary to find and keep a job, e.g., self-respect, responsibility, work ethic, punctuality, respect for authority, interviewing. In addition, some ministries also provide additional training in welding, carpentry, cooking, or auto repair, for example.

Some jobs preparedness ministries recruit local businesses to provide employment opportunities for the program participants. One option for you to consider is the *Work Life* program, a set of biblically based jobs preparedness resources that the Chalmers Center has developed in partnership with Jobs for Life (www.jobsforlife.org) and Advance Memphis (www.advancememphis.org). In addition, Jobs for Life has additional resources that can help you with a jobs preparedness ministry.

Chapters 3–5 of this book have outlined the policies, procedures, and tools that your church can use in its benevolence work. In the midst of discussing forms, exercises, and protocols, do not forget that each person who approaches your church for assistance has a unique story— a story of both dignity and brokenness, a story of immense complexity and nuance. As chapter 2 highlighted, a multitude of factors contribute to material poverty, so applying these principles and procedures to real people is not always a straightforward process. *Thus, your actions must always be rooted in prayer, wisdom, and a heart of humility, recognizing that poverty alleviation is a miraculous work of Jesus Christ, who is restoring what is broken in all of us.*

TASKS TO COMPLETE: *Consider Existing and New Church Ministries*

• *Consider the existing ministries of your church—including your church's "ordinary" ministry. Can you use them to strengthen your benevolence ministry? List several steps you will take to link these ministries to your benevolence work.*

• *Think of some new ministries your church might undertake. Would a financial education ministry or a jobs preparedness ministry be a good option for the people you are serving? Explore the extent to which these ministries already exist in your community. Would it be better for you to link to these existing ministries or to start a new one?*

EXPLORE ONLINE RESOURCES

Create an account on the Chalmers Center's User Portal to access some of the tools and resources mentioned in this chapter.

Create an Account At:
www.helpingwithouthurting.org/benevolence

Enter Access Code: walkwith

CHAPTER 6

RUBBER MEETS THE ROAD

TRAINING SCENARIOS AND QUESTIONS

Given the complexity of poverty, even carefully formed policies and procedures have to be applied on a case-by-case basis.

No two people who approach your church for assistance will be exactly the same. Although this truth may sound daunting, it also gives us an opportunity to learn how to depend more deeply on God, walking with Him as He does His work in us and in the person we are seeking to help.

This chapter contains a number of short scenarios, most of which are based on actual stories churches or ministries have shared with us. They provide a chance for your benevolence team to discuss how you might respond to various situations, and they might be a helpful tool to use when orienting and training volunteers or new members of your team.

While the purpose of these scenarios is to help you to apply the principles of asset-based, participatory poverty alleviation, there is more than one healthy way to address each of these situations. Walking with people developmentally is as much an art as it is a science. So while you should try to apply the principles in this book, at the core of the process is listening—not just for information—but also for attitudes, emotions, fears, and hopes. *In what direction are this person's head and heart seemingly pointed?* And you must also be listening to God by being deeply rooted in Scripture and praying for the guidance of the Holy Spirit as you seek to truly help the individual or family.

At the end of each scenario are a few questions for your team to discuss, followed by a few thoughts on how I (Steve) might approach each of the situations presented. My reflections are by no means definitive or authoritative. They are simply intended to provide one perspective for your team to discuss as you seek to learn and grow together.

SCENARIO 1: SHARON

Sharon, a single twenty-one-year-old, calls a deacon in your church. She works as a cashier at a local gas station, and a coworker, Tom, had given her the deacon's phone number. Tom, twenty, is a member of your church, and he has worked with Sharon for close to a year. He has been sharing the gospel with her and has invited her to come to church with him many times, but she never has. Upon learning of her financial struggles, Tom encouraged Sharon to call a deacon and request assistance. Tom is hopeful that by connecting Sharon with the deacons, she will begin to attend the church.

The deacon agrees to meet with Sharon after church on Sunday to hear more details about her situation. Sharon comes to church and is warmly welcomed by several people in the congregation. She meets with the deacon and explains that she is going to be short on rent for the third month in a row. She is also two months behind on her electric bill.

In total, Sharon needs $1,100 to catch up. The deacon learns that Sharon graduated from high school but did not pursue college. She lived at home after high school, but due to significant conflict with her parents, she has been on her own for the past year. Besides monthly cost-of-living expenses, Sharon will have a monthly car payment of $300 for another two years.

Questions for you to consider:

1. Will failure to provide immediate assistance likely result in serious harm?

2. Is Sharon largely responsible for her situation?

3. What further information would you want to know about her before determining how to proceed?

4. What possible changes or ways of moving forward in life would you want to discuss with her?

5. What actions will you take that could contribute to the long-term goal of empowering Sharon to live in right relationship with God, self, others, and the rest of creation?

STEVE'S REFLECTIONS

Sharon is not in a situation in which a lack of immediate aid will cause her serious harm. She might get evicted, which would be unfortunate and inconvenient, but it will not put her in danger.

In addition, it appears that Sharon is largely responsible for her situation, as she is simply living beyond her means. I believe that truly loving Sharon means helping her own the situation by encouraging her to address the actions that got her into these problems. Providing immediate assistance to Sharon could undermine this ownership, thereby disempowering her from truly making progress in her life.

If I were the deacon who first meets with Sharon, I would communicate that the church benevolence team works with people to help them avoid ongoing financial problems. Except in the case of emergencies, the church does not provide immediate material assistance. Instead, it works with people through a mutually created action plan that details what the person and the church will do to help the person with their financial life.

The first step in that process is working through an intake form. I would show Sharon the form and see if she would be interested in taking the next step, explaining that although the church will not provide $1,100 to cover her rent and utility payments, we would love to work with her as she looks into ways to pay this debt and avoid future financial troubles. This process would include creating an action plan that would walk Sharon through the process of setting goals and achieving those goals. The church would provide encouragement, counsel, limited financial help as appropriate, and link her with other organizations that could assist her with specific goals.

I would tell Sharon of the range or maximum amount of financial assistance we could possibly give, according to our policies. In addition, I would let her know that our church only provides funds as the person takes steps forward as outlined in their action plan. The funds usually come in stages and/or when the plan is fully completed, but not upfront.

Note that if we pay the bulk of funds the church policy allows right away, Sharon may very well take the money and run, and an opportunity to walk more deeply with her will be lost.

If Sharon is willing to begin the process of pursuing long-term financial stability rather than just immediate material assistance, she will need to tackle a number of challenges. Several of these challenges might crop up when creating the action plan:

- She may need to lower her housing costs. Because it is hard for a single person at a low-paying job to afford to live alone, Sharon may need to get a roommate.

- She may need to consider selling her car and get more affordable transportation, as her monthly car payment is rather large. Are mass transit or biking feasible options in her community?

- Sharon might benefit from the financial education discussed in chapter 5, particularly since she is young and just starting out. Even though she currently has a low-paying job, learning how to steward those limited resources and evaluate her spending patterns would be a crucial step in pursuing financial stability.

- Sharon should consider developing skills to qualify for better long-term employment. This might mean going to school or doing some kind of job certification training. The local community college or technical institute might be a good start, but it will require careful time management, a skill that the encourager in our church could help her cultivate and implement.

- Eventually, Sharon should consider addressing her relationship with her parents. Identifying what has gone sour in that relationship, why it has gone wrong, and whether reconciliation is possible are part of Sharon's creating a support system and moving back into right relationship with them.

My key message to Sharon would be that struggling to meet her bills is probably not going to be a one-time issue, unless she takes steps to change the underlying factors contributing to her material poverty. Sharon may be in a cycle of repeated financial turmoil, so immediately helping her pay the bills would not really be helping her to move forward in life. Instead, I would offer to come alongside Sharon in doing the long-term work of addressing the underlying issues that led to her present circumstances. If Sharon is not interested, I would tell her that we could not provide her with any financial assistance at this time.

I would also touch base with Tom and talk through the assistance I offered Sharon—as well as the basics of whether or not she accepted that offer. I would want Tom to be on board with the direction that the church is taking, so he could provide a consistent voice of support and encouragement in her day-to-day life. If the church has done a good job of communicating its benevolence vision and policies to the congregation, Tom would enthusiastically support the church's approach to Sharon.

SCENARIO 2: DAVID AND LINDA

David and Linda are married and have four children between the ages of nine and fifteen. David has a checkered work history. His dream is to make a living as a musician. He has tried numerous times to make this dream a reality, sometimes working part-time at a low-paying job, and other times fully pursuing a career in music. While he has had some music opportunities that have paid well, he has never earned enough from music to provide for his family and pay the bills consistently.

Through the years, David and Linda have attended various churches and have received help paying their bills numerous times. They have been in your church for five years. While David has not attended very often the past two years, Linda is a fairly consistent attendee. She ensures that her children participate in church, Sunday school, and the youth group.

Four years ago, David and Linda came to the church asking for help to pay some bills. This request went directly to the pastor, and the pastor made a deal with David that if he would attend a jobs preparedness training program the church was hosting, the church would help with a few rent and utility bills. David faithfully participated in the twelve-week training. During the training, he was able to identify many skills he could use to support his family, as well as several obstacles that prevented him from providing for them.

At the end of the job preparedness training, David secured a job with a local retailer. While the pay was not high and he did not find the work very fulfilling, David and Linda were able to cover their bills through his salary.

While working at the retailer, David was diagnosed with bipolar disorder. This helped explain many of his emotional ups and downs and especially his tendency to impulsively quit jobs in favor of relaunching his music career.

After over two years working at the retailer, David stopped taking his medication and suddenly quit his job, announcing that he was going to go back to work as a musician. Within a few months, David and Linda were again struggling to pay their bills.

Throughout David's struggles to provide for his family, Linda worked a few odd jobs here and there. But because of her desire to homeschool their children, she turned down several work opportunities. Their financial struggles have caused significant strain on their marriage and parenting throughout the years.

David has come back to the church asking for help with rent money once again.

Questions for you to consider:

1. Will failure to provide immediate assistance likely result in serious harm?

2. Are David and Linda largely responsible for their situation?

3. What further information would you want to know about them before determining how to proceed?

4. What possible changes or ways of moving forward in life would you want to discuss with them?

5. What actions will you take that could contribute to the long-term goal of empowering David and Linda to live in right relationship with God, self, others, and the rest of creation?

STEVE'S REFLECTIONS

David and Linda are not in danger of serious harm. In addition, although David's bipolar disorder presents special challenges, for the most part, the couple is responsible for their financial situation. David and Linda are generally able-bodied people and have basic job skills, but they are not willing to work at the types of jobs that could provide for them and their children. Because they both profess to be followers of Christ, they need to obey the biblical command to provide for their family through their work. I believe it would be a mistake to provide immediate financial help with paying their bills, because doing so would reinforce an ongoing pattern of financial dependency.

But this does not mean there is nothing I would do to help David and Linda. On the contrary, I would want to walk with them as they tackle some important issues:

- David needs to relook at his medical issues and bipolar diagnosis. Why did he stop taking his medication? Would going back to the doctor and/or seeing a counselor be helpful?

- Linda needs to consider bringing some income into the home through a part-time job, for even if David works full-time, he will probably not earn enough to cover all their expenses.

- Marriage counseling would also be helpful for David and Linda. If they are willing to pursue counseling, the church should consider covering part of those expenses as David and Linda work to break out of their cycle of material poverty. This could be a good way to use the church's financial resources to support lasting change in their lives.

It will take some time to explore all the issues and possibilities with David and Linda. At this point, I would explain the process the church uses to help people—i.e., gathering relevant information and forming an action plan—and then I would ask David and Linda if they wanted to pursue this with me. Because of their long history of getting help from churches in addition to ours, I would not provide financial help initially but would wait to see them demonstrate some consistency in carrying out the steps in their action plan.

SCENARIO 3: SHERRY

Sherry walks into your church office, holding her little boy's hand. She lives in the apartment complex down the street from your church. She has a red welt on her cheek and the beginnings of a black eye. Sherry tearfully tells the church secretary that her husband is on one of his drunken rages. He hit her—which is nothing new—and for the first time he tried to hit their son. When Sherry stood in her husband's way to stop him from hitting their little boy, her husband punched her hard in the eye. Sherry is very afraid that her husband will try to track her down. She asks if the church could help her.

Questions for you to consider:

1. Will failure to provide immediate assistance likely result in serious harm?

2. Is Sherry largely responsible for her situation?

3. What further information would you want to know about her before determining how to proceed?

4. What possible changes or ways of moving forward in life would you want to discuss with her?

5. What actions will you take that could contribute to the long-term goal of empowering Sherry to live in right relationship with God, self, others, and the rest of creation?

STEVE'S REFLECTIONS

Sherry and her son are victims of domestic abuse and are in danger. The church needs to act immediately. The church secretary knows the church's benevolence policies, so she is able to assure Sherry that the church can help her. If somebody on the benevolence team is available, they should be called in at this point. If they are not available, they should at least be contacted by phone.

If I were the benevolence team member who was called in, I would see if Sherry needed to go to the doctor or the emergency room, taking her there if needed. Furthermore, I would encourage Sherry to allow me to contact the police on her behalf. She will need to discuss the incident with them and consider pressing charges. In addition, if Sherry needs to go home to get clothes or other items, the police will need to go with her to ensure her safety.

I would inform Sherry that, at the very least, our church will be able to pay for a hotel room and food for several days, until we are able to develop a longer-term plan together.

Finally, I would contact a woman on our benevolence team or in our pool of volunteers to be the main point person for Sherry through this entire process.

It may be that this incident becomes a trigger for Sherry to change the dynamics in her family in order to rid her home of violence. If so, then we need to be ready to take the next steps with her. These steps could include obtaining a restraining order and/or seeking court intervention to mandate alcohol and anger management counseling for her husband. Ideally, this would lead to inroads into his life as well.

Once her husband becomes sober, there is also a possibility that Sherry may return to her situation without taking any steps to prevent this from happening again. While we do not have the right to stop this, we need to assure Sherry that the church wants to help her to create a safer and more stable home for herself and her son. And she needs to know that she can call the church at any time she is fearful for her or her son's safety.

SCENARIO 4: KATHY[1]

Kathy is a forty-year-old divorced mother of three children. Her ex-husband was abusive to both her and the kids. Following the divorce, Kathy lived with her mother, who has a history of relying on agencies and churches for financial assistance. Kathy's mother is controlling and views Kathy as a "problem child" who was a "slow learner" and could not take care of herself. Kathy's father was an alcoholic, and he verbally and physically abused both Kathy and her mother for many years until his death.

Your benevolence team has been walking with Kathy for over a year, encouraging her to complete her action plan and providing some financial assistance. Progress has been up and down. Just when you think she is on the verge of moving forward, another setback occurs or she does not follow through with what she was supposed to do. Yet there have been some positive changes in her life. Kathy was able to move out of her mother's home and into her own apartment a year ago. She had been paying her mother $300 in rent, but now her government-subsidized apartment costs only $125 per month. Kathy began working at a good job, but she injured her back and is now unable to work.

At present, Kathy's main source of income is the $800 per month she receives from worker's compensation due to her injury at work. She says that she also receives $40 a month in food stamps but that she never sees this money because it goes toward paying down what she owes as restitution for welfare fraud. This sounds suspicious to the volunteers working with her, and they have not been able to verify this information. Kathy also receives some child support money from her ex-husband, but this is intermittent.

The volunteers know that Kathy needs help and support, but they are also frustrated with her. Kathy doesn't cooperate with seemingly simple and straightforward steps to help herself. For example, volunteers have set up appointments to talk with her in more detail, but she cancels, does not show up, or leaves early. And when asked to bring financial records to work on a budget, she fails to bring the correct information.

In addition, the volunteers suspect that Kathy is not being completely truthful. She has told volunteers different stories about her past and her situation. And there are discrepancies between the information that Kathy gives about her food stamps and the information received from the local welfare office about its policies.

Kathy has a number of physical and mental health issues. She is a recovering alcoholic and takes medications for her back pain, depression, anxiety, and diabetes.

Protective Services is involved because the children have not been attending school on a consistent basis. As a result of their absenteeism, two of the children are struggling academically. Protective Services has recommended counseling for both Kathy and the children, but she has not followed through on either of these.

To add to the burden and complexity, Kathy's ten-year-old daughter confided in one of the volunteers, "I don't want to grow up to be like my mother."

The frustrated volunteers approach your benevolence team, wondering if there is any point in continuing to walk with Kathy.

Questions for you to consider:

1. Will failure to provide immediate assistance likely result in serious harm?

2. Is Kathy largely responsible for her situation?

3. What further information would you want to know about Kathy before determining how to proceed?

4. What possible changes or ways of moving forward in life would you want to discuss with Kathy?

5. What actions will you take that could contribute to the long-term goal of empowering Kathy to live in right relationship with God, self, others, and the rest of creation?

STEVE'S REFLECTIONS

The issue in this case is not about providing immediate financial assistance; rather the issue is whether or not the church should continue to walk with Kathy, providing ongoing encouragement and accountability along with occasional financial support.

Determining Kathy's responsibility for causing her situation is complicated. At one level, Kathy is the person who is primarily responsible for her circumstances, and she needs to be the main agent for making positive changes in her life. But there are also factors in Kathy's past that might be behind some of her unhealthy patterns of behavior: she struggles with alcohol addiction, which she likely inherited from her father; her mother has always been negative about her; and both Kathy's father and husband were abusive. It is likely that Kathy is suffering from trauma.

Finding a way to help Kathy to get counseling and to follow through on appointments with your volunteers would be a high priority in Kathy's process of transformation. But as mentioned in chapter 2, when walking alongside people who have experienced trauma, we must be careful not to be too dictatorial, demanding, or controlling. If Kathy's past experiences have made her feel helpless and powerless, an aggressive approach might be counterproductive.

There is no easy solution for Kathy. Counseling, friendly encouragers, and gentle discipling relationships that do not make strong demands are good ongoing steps. In time, we might be able to move toward suggesting more focused changes in her financial life.

We should recognize that this process will likely be long and hard, as Kathy might have very deep wounds. This is a situation where leading with empathy is crucial. That empathy would temper some of the natural frustration the church and volunteers experience when Kathy does not follow through on her promises or undermines her progress. I would recommend that our church continue to walk with Kathy, providing occasional financial assistance within the dollar amounts set by our church's benevolence policies.

SCENARIO 5: JEANINE

Jeanine is in her early sixties and works full-time as a cafeteria worker at the local high school. As much as she is physically able, she also works at a fast-food restaurant a few weekends per month. Jeanine has three grown sons. One is serving a prison term of four years and periodically asks her for money to pay for a phone card and miscellaneous expenses within the prison. The second son chooses to work only sporadically as a landscaper and is often short on funds. He frequently asks Jeanine for help, which she provides as much as she can. Jeanine's third son, who is in his late twenties, works full-time and lives at home with her, but he contributes nothing to paying for the household's expenses.

Jeanine's husband left her fifteen years ago, so she has had to raise her sons and provide for herself throughout that time.

Neither Jeanine nor her sons have a previous relationship with the church; she just heard about your church and called to see if there was any way that the church could help her with some bills that are due.

Her biggest financial challenge appears to be that she has fallen behind on mortgage payments on the house in which she has lived for the past twenty years.

Questions for you to consider:

1. Will failure to provide immediate assistance likely result in serious harm?

2. Is Jeanine largely responsible for her situation?

3. What further information would you want to know about Jeanine before determining how to proceed?

4. What possible changes or ways of moving forward in life would you want to discuss with Jeanine?

5. What actions will you take that could contribute to the long-term goal of empowering Jeanine to live in right relationship with God, self, others, and the rest of creation?

STEVE'S REFLECTIONS

While Jeanine is not in danger of serious physical harm, it is important to quickly find out if her house is in danger of going into foreclosure. If so, immediate steps need to be taken, as losing this asset would create further financial problems.

Jeanine is clearly a hard worker. She is doing her best to provide for herself and to love her sons. It is unlikely that providing immediate and temporary financial assistance will plunge her into dependency. In addition, helping her with this immediate problem may open the door to a longer-term relationship with your church.

A first step would be working with Jeanine and her mortgage company to fully understand her situation. If foreclosure is imminent, I would ask the mortgage company to hold off on foreclosure and/or make a mortgage payment on her behalf.

As part of addressing the underlying factors contributing to her financial struggles, I would want to have conversations with Jeanine about what it really means to love her sons. She certainly should cut back on providing financial assistance to the son who works on-and-off by choice. I would also explore why the son who is living with her and has a full-time job is not contributing money to cover living expenses. Finally, I might inquire as to whether or not the son who is in prison is spending his money wisely.

If Jeanine expresses a desire to move forward in the development process, she would benefit from the type of financial education described in chapter 5. In the course of creating a budget and tracking expenses, she could see and evaluate how much of her income is going toward her sons.

As the relationship with Jeanine deepens, I would probably ask to meet with the son who is living with her. Depending on how the meeting goes, he could join Jeanine in financial education training. Jeanine could include his wages in the budgeting process as part of the household income, and I would encourage her to present the budget to him as a challenge for him to contribute financially. Jeanine needs to grow to the point where she sees it as both a loving and natural thing to request that he help cover the household expenses. And he needs to see that it is abnormal and unloving to not consistently contribute financially, at least by paying rent.

I would expect Jeanine to need significant emotional support if she alters her financial support for her sons. Her sons are likely to resist these changes, and the church and Jeanine's encouragers should be prepared for her to struggle with guilt and sadness about making such a hard decision. I would look for women in the church who would support Jeanine and stand with her—otherwise, she might let her sons convince her to return to the same unhealthy patterns.

SCENARIO 6: DONOVAN AND SANDRA

Donovan and Sandra have been married for fifteen years and have a nine-year-old daughter and a seven-year-old son. They have been members of your church for eight years and are very active: they teach Sunday school, volunteer often, and are heavily involved in a small group.

Donovan and Sandra live in a rural area, eight miles from town and twenty miles from the manufacturing plant where Donovan works full-time. Sandra, who historically has worked at various fast-food restaurants, stopped working a year ago in order to go back to college to get her elementary education degree. They have utilized all the available options for scholarships and financial aid, enabling them to find a way to pay for Sandra's education. While things are financially doable, money will be very tight until Sandra graduates in two years. Unfortunately, the transmission on their only car died and needs to be rebuilt. The price tag is $2,500, and they are $1,000 short. They ask your church for financial assistance.

Questions for you to consider:

1. Will failure to provide immediate assistance likely result in serious harm?

2. Are Donovan and Sandra largely responsible for their situation?

3. What further information would you want to know about them before determining how to proceed?

4. What possible changes or ways of moving forward in life would you want to discuss with them?

5. What actions will you take that could contribute to the long-term goal of empowering Donovan and Sandra to live in right relationship with God, self, others, and the rest of creation?

STEVE'S REFLECTIONS

Not having transportation will not cause immediate serious harm. However, since Donovan and Sandra live in a rural area, there is no public transportation and no carpools are available. So not getting the car fixed quickly will cause all sorts of problems. If Donovan cannot get to work and Sandra cannot get to school, it will undermine their family's current and future income. Immediate action is worth considering.

While Donovan and Sandra should have enough emergency funds set aside to handle this kind of situation, their being short $1,000 is understandable, especially given their investment of time and money into Sandra's education. I do not see them as principally responsible for their unexpected dilemma.

In addition, Donovan and Sandra are clearly hardworking people who are trying to improve their lives. It is unlikely that one-time financial assistance will plunge them into dependency.

Thus, I would be generous with them. I would pay the $1,000, and I would also ask them if coming up with the other $1,500 is going to completely deplete their emergency fund. If so, I would offer to pay a bit more than the $1,000 so that they are not left completely financially vulnerable.

Donovan and Sandra's faithful involvement in the church would inform this offer of significant financial help. It is not that they have "earned" help, as if the church were a bank that they can withdraw from. But there is a sense in which they have faithfully labored in and loved the church. In turn, I would see this as an opportunity to labor and love alongside of them.

SCENARIO 7: MARIA

Maria is eighteen years old and walks into your church's office. She has a two-year-old son and a newborn daughter. The church secretary talks with Maria for a few minutes, and then goes to the pastor's office and suggests that he talk with Maria. Maria tells the pastor and secretary that she moved to town three months ago with her boyfriend, who is the father of her newborn. Two weeks ago, the boyfriend took off without warning. She has called and texted him many times, but he is not responding. Maria says she has enough money for this month's rent, utilities, and food, but that is all she has.

Maria reveals that she dropped out of high school when her first child was born. She lived with a few different boyfriends on and off. A year ago she spent three months in a program for homeless women with children. She says she left that program because the staff was mean and unfair to her. After that she worked in various part-time jobs until she met her most recent boyfriend. Since then she has primarily been staying at home with the children, living on what her boyfriend supplied and on government benefits. Maria indicates that she would like to stay in the area and establish a new life.

Your pastor asks Maria to come to church that Sunday and to meet with a deacon and his wife after the service. He says that your church will provide lunch and someone to watch her children, enabling her to have a focused time with the deacon and his wife. The pastor calls the deacon and lets him know the basics of Maria's situation. On Sunday, Maria recounts her story and asks if there is anything the church can do to help her start a new life.

With the help of the deacon and his wife, Maria creates a three-month action plan with four goals: (1) get a job; (2) find childcare; (3) obtain affordable housing; and (4) work on her GED.

The church helps Maria get a job at a local company. The wages are ten dollars per hour, and the job provides health benefits. Two women in the church agree to provide childcare on a rotating basis so Maria can work. Maria pays a third of the cost for this childcare, the church pays another third, and the two women donate the other third by charging a discounted rate. Another member of the church who owns several apartments agrees to rent to Maria at half of the market value for one year—as long as she meets the goals of her action plan with the church. Finally, after the three months of settling in, Maria starts taking GED classes offered by a local nonprofit. While not required, Maria also starts attending the church regularly. Maria seems to be working hard to turn her life around. She constantly expresses gratitude to the church and to the various members who are walking alongside of her.

One day, Maria's employer calls the head of the benevolence committee to let him know that he caught Maria stealing from the cash register. Further investigation reveals that she has done this numerous times over the past month. Maria confessed that she took the extra money because her boyfriend showed up six weeks ago and is now living with her. He is not working, so she needs extra money to cover his expenses. She kept all this secret because her lease prohibits her from having extra guests for more than two weeks without the landlord's permission. Maria is panicking, because she fears her behavior is going to cause her to lose her job and her housing. She seems genuinely repentant and ashamed of her actions.

Questions for you to consider:

1. Will failure to provide immediate assistance likely result in serious harm?

2. Is Maria largely responsible for her situation?

3. What further information would you want to know about her before determining how to proceed?

4. What possible changes or ways of moving forward in life would you want to discuss with her?

5. What actions will you take that could contribute to the long-term goal of empowering Maria to live in right relationship with God, self, others, and the rest of creation?

STEVE'S REFLECTIONS

Many great things are happening in Maria's life. With the church's assistance, she has started to make progress. She has been faithfully working and getting involved in the church, and she has exhibited an attitude of thankfulness and optimism. Maria seems sincerely open to change, which may have been triggered by the crisis of her boyfriend leaving.

But now she has messed up. She is very young, so she is still maturing into adulthood. She is clearly trying. I would not give up on Maria. God doesn't give up on us that easily!

First, I would talk with Maria's employer and ask if he is willing to let her continue working in a role that does not involve easy access to money. It is crucial that Maria be required to gradually pay back what she stole, so I would work jointly with Maria and the employer to determine how much she will repay each month.

Second, the living situation needs to be addressed. I would ask the landlord to show Maria mercy for violating the rules. Before making this request, I would make sure that Maria agrees that the boyfriend will be out by a specified date. This is only fair to the landlord, and our church would not want to provide financial support for unmarried people to live together. I would dig deeper into conversations with Maria and her boyfriend about their relationship, looking for opportunities to counsel them about God's design for marriage. In addition, I would try to listen to the hopes and fears they express. If the boyfriend is open to starting afresh, I would create an action plan with him that includes our working together to find affordable housing so that he no longer needs to live with Maria.

Walking with Maria will likely be a bumpy road. Above all, I would communicate that forgiveness and mercy are real and that the church will stick with her in light of her repentant attitude. If she is not already involved in a small group, this would be the time to encourage her to join one. Maria needs as many supportive and encouraging people in her life as possible, and she needs to learn about both God's grace and her calling to live according to His standards for her life. This time in Maria's life is a window of opportunity—I would not want to miss it.

SCENARIO 8: TORI

Tori is a single, thirty-year-old mom who has been sporadically attending your church for the past two years. Her daughter, Katie, is fourteen. For the past few years, Katie has come faithfully to your church and has also attended the youth group. Six months ago, Katie publically professed her faith in Christ and became a member of your church.

Tori recently broke up with her live-in boyfriend. She is not working, and it is hard to determine if she has ever held a steady job. Tori was a stay-at-home mom when she was married, and she has had a string of live-in boyfriends over the past six years since her divorce. She is trying to get classified as disabled, stating she has cancer and is too weak and tired to work. However, Tori does not appear to be ill, and she is fully capable of working.

As you talk with Tori, it becomes clear that she sees securing government disability benefits as the long-term solution to her financial instability. Becky, a member of your church who has befriended Katie, has visited Tori's house numerous times, expressing her care and inviting Tori to come to church. Becky thinks that Tori might be inaccurately representing her health condition. Becky has encouraged Tori to look for work, but Tori has consistently refused to do so. During one of Becky's last visits, Tori says that she is $700 short for this month's rent and utilities. The rent is due in three days, and the utilities are due in a week. She wants to see if the church would pay them for her. This is the first time Tori has asked for help from the church.

Questions for you to consider:

1. Will failure to provide immediate assistance likely result in serious harm?

2. Is Tori largely responsible for her situation?

3. What further information would you want to know about her before determining how to proceed?

4. What possible changes or ways of moving forward in life would you want to discuss with her?

5. What actions will you take that could contribute to the long-term goal of empowering Tori to live in right relationship with God, self, others, and the rest of creation?

STEVE'S REFLECTIONS

Tori is not in danger of serious harm, and she is also primarily responsible for her situation.

I would explain to Tori that the church benevolence team works with people to help them avoid ongoing financial problems, describing both the intake form and action plan process.

If Tori is willing to proceed, I would explore with her the possibility of a joint meeting with a representative from the church and Tori's caseworker at the government benefits office. This meeting would provide a better sense of Tori's physical capacity and would clarify if she is truly likely to qualify for disability assistance from the government. I would work with Tori to use the information from this meeting to create an action plan that would help her move forward in life.

If Tori completes the creation of the action plan, I would offer to pay part of the upcoming rent and utility bills—but not all of them. Determining the amount of financial assistance would depend on what other resources Tori has available. Helping in some tangible way with her current bills could help reinforce the church's care for her and Katie. But refusing to pay the entire bill communicates that Tori needs to be actively engaged in her own improvement—and it communicates that the church will not just automatically help her with expenses if she makes no effort to improve her situation.

Katie has been quiet concerning her mother's health. I would communicate with Katie that the church is eager and willing to help her mom to find long-term solutions. Katie is mature for her age and has great relationships with many people in your church. I would continually let her know that the church is actively seeking to help. If Tori refuses the church's offer to walk with her over time, I would not want Katie to feel rejected or discarded by the church. I would let Katie know that the church will be there for her if she finds herself in a dangerous or unhealthy situation. Katie's view of the church, her family, and herself are currently being shaped, and I would want the church to have a voice in her life moving forward.

EPILOGUE: GET MOVING!

As mentioned in the introduction, we readily admit that this book is not the final word on this important subject. The truth is that there are still many unknowns in benevolence work, so we see this resource as part of a living project, a project that you can speak into as you use this guide. Please share encouraging stories and suggestions for improvement with us at benevolence@chalmers.org.

We have covered a lot of ground in this book, trying to prepare you for the complexity of implementing an effective benevolence ministry. But don't be overwhelmed by all of these concepts and tools. Remember that ultimately *this is God's work, not ours.* He is the one who is restoring all things. He is the author of change. And He is the one who can alleviate poverty. The success or failure of His cosmic plan is not contingent on whether or not we perfectly engage in poverty alleviation. In fact, we never will do it perfectly! *The joy is that God does not require perfection from us; rather, He asks us to be faithful servants who learn from our mistakes.* When we let fear of doing it wrong lead us into paralysis, we are letting our god-complexes get in the way. We are acting as though our actions are the ultimate determiner of success, rather than the God who can use our humble—albeit imperfect—service for His glory and kingdom.

So get moving. Bathe your benevolence work in prayer, love, humility, and discernment. Move forward in walking alongside the Bens and Debbies who come to your church, seeking to be ambassadors of reconciliation in their lives. And rejoice that one day God will complete the work He has started—in the Bens, in the Debbies, and in all of us.

—Steve Corbett and Brian Fikkert

NOTES

Introduction

1. Steve Corbett and Brian Fikkert, *When Helping Hurts: How to Alleviate Poverty without Hurting the Poor . . . and Yourself* (Chicago: Moody, 2012).

Chapter 1: Reframing Benevolence

1. In *When Helping Hurts* we discussed *individual behaviors* and *systemic injustice* as causes of broken relationships. Here we have divided *systemic injustice* into *abusive or exploitive people* and *oppressive systems*. We have also included *demonic forces* here, which we underemphasized in *When Helping Hurts*. As North Americans, we authors have been influenced by Western materialism and tend to forget the spiritual forces that are at work in the world. For further discussion about these issues, see chapters 5–7 in Brian Fikkert and Russell Mask, *From Dependence to Dignity: How to Alleviate Poverty through Church-Centered Microfinance* (Grand Rapids: Zondervan, 2015).
2. "Eric," interview by Katie Casselberry, February 12, 2015.
3. Ibid.
4. This is a modification of the definition of paternalism found in Roland Bunch, *Two Ears of Corn: A Guide to People-Centered Agricultural Improvement* (Oklahoma City: World Neighbors, 1982), 19–23.
5. "James," interview by Katie Casselberry, March 11, 2015.
6. Throughout church history, these have been referred to as the "ordinary means of grace." Some churches add several other items to the list, and some subtract "prayer." For a helpful introduction to this topic, see Luke Stamps, "Especially Preaching: The Ordinary Means of Grace and Christian Spirituality," The Gospel Coalition, February 10, 2011, accessed May 28, 2015, http://thegospelcoalition.org/article/especially-preaching-the-ordinary-means-of-grace-and-christian-spirituality.

Chapter 2: Take a Second Look

1. Center for Substance Abuse Treatment (US), "Trauma-Informed Care: A Sociocultural Perspective," in *Trauma-Informed Care in Behavioral Health Services*, Treatment Improvement Protocol (TIP) Series 57, HHS Publication No. (SMA) 13–4801 (Rockville, MD: Substance Abuse and Mental Health Services Administration, 2014), accessed May 15, 2015, http://www.ncbi.nlm.nih.gov/books/NBK207195/.
2. Angela Browne and Shari S. Bassuk, "Intimate Violence in the Lives of Homeless and Poor Housed Women: Prevalence and Patterns in an Ethnically Diverse Sample," *American Journal of Orthopsychiatry* 6, no. 2 (April 1997): 270, 273.
3. Kathryn Collins, Kay Connors, Sara Davis, April Donohue, Sarah Gardner, Erica Goldblatt, Anna Hayward, Laurel Kiser, Fred Strieder, and Elizabeth Thompson, *Understanding the Impact of Trauma and Urban Poverty on Family Systems:*

Risks, Resilience, and Interventions (Baltimore: Family Informed Trauma Treatment Center, 2010), 4, accessed May 15, 2015, www.nctsn.org/sites/default/files/assets/pdfs/understanding_the_impact_of_trauma.pdf.

4. Ibid.

5. Center for Substance Abuse Treatment (US), "Trauma-Informed Care: A Sociocultural Perspective."

6. Collins et al., *Understanding the Impact of Trauma and Urban Poverty on Family Systems*, 23.

7. If you are interested in learning more about the long-term effects of childhood trauma, see the ongoing *Adverse Childhood Experiences Study* conducted by the Centers for Disease Control and Prevention and Kaiser Permanente in San Diego: www.acestudy.org.

8. Lizabeth Roamer and Leslie Lebowitz, "Understanding Severe Traumatization," in *Mental Health & Experts Manual*, 6th ed. (Frankfort, KY: Kentucky Department of Public Advocacy, 2002), accessed May 15, 2015, http://www.dpa.state.ky.us/library/manuals/mental/Ch27.html.

9. Ibid.

10. Center for Substance Abuse Treatment (US), "Trauma-Informed Care: A Sociocultural Perspective."

11. Robert D. Putnam, *Our Kids: The American Dream in Crisis* (New York: Simon & Schuster, 2015).

12. Ibid., 110–11.

13. Betty Hart and Todd R. Risley, *Meaningful Differences in the Everyday Experience of Young American Children* (Baltimore: Paul H. Brookes, 1995) as cited in Putnam, *Our Kids*, 116.

14. Ibid, as cited in Putnam, *Our Kids*, 121.

15. For a helpful summary, see Collins et al., *Understanding the Impact of Trauma and Urban Poverty on Family Systems*.

16. Sendhil Mullainathan, "Racial Bias, Even When We Have Good Intentions," *New York Times*, January 3, 2015, accessed June 16, 2015, http://www.nytimes.com/2015/01/04/upshot/the-measuring-sticks-of-racial-bias-.html?_r=0.

17. E. J. R. David, ed., *Internalized Oppression: The Psychology of Marginalized Groups* (New York: Springer Publishing Company, 2013); E. J. R. David, *Brown Skin, White Minds: Filipino- / American Postcolonial Psychology* (Charlotte, NC: Information Age Publishing, 2013).

Chapter 3: Built for Transformation

1. This tool draws on Diaconal Ministries Canada, "Guidelines for Benevolence," accessed May 28, 2015, http://diaconalministries.com/wp-content/uploads/2014/01/Guidelines-for-Benevolence-1.pdf.

2. "James," interview by Katie Casselberry, March 11, 2015.

3. "Eric," interview by Katie Casselberry, February 12, 2015.

4. "Nate," interview by Katie Casselberry, November 3, 2015.

5. Consumer Financial Protection Bureau as quoted in Susanna Montezemolo, *Payday Lending Abuses and Predatory Practices: The State of Lending in America & Its*

Impact on U.S. Households (Durham, NC: Center for Responsible Lending, September 2013).

6. For more on the pitfalls of churches making loans, see Brian Fikkert and Russell Mask, *From Dependence to Dignity: How to Alleviate Poverty through Church-Centered Microfinance* (Grand Rapids: Zondervan, 2015).

7. See chapter 8 of Steve Corbett and Brian Fikkert, *When Helping Hurts: How to Alleviate Poverty without Hurting the Poor . . . and Yourself* (Chicago: Moody, 2012).

8. "Nate," interview.

9. The idea of starting small and succeeding can be found in Roland Bunch, *Two Ears of Corn: A Guide to People-Centered Agricultural Improvement* (Oklahoma City: World Neighbors, 1982), 21–36.

Chapter 4: From Electric Bill to Restoration

1. "Eric," interview by Katie Casselberry, February 12, 2015.

2. With the exception of the budget from section 3 and the majority of section 4, this tool is adapted and expanded with permission from Redeemer Presbyterian Church, "Intake Form," in *The Redeemer Presbyterian Church Diaconate Manual: A Handbook for Diaconate Mercy Ministry*, 3rd ed. (New York: RPC Press, 2001).

3. From J. Mark Bowers, *Faith & Finances*, ed. Jerilyn Sanders, Sam Moore, and Amy Kuenzel (Chattanooga: The Chalmers Center, 2012), 105.

4. "Nate," interview by Katie Casselberry, February 17, 2015.

5. This tool is adapted and expanded with permission from Diaconal Ministries Canada, "Guidelines for Benevolence," accessed May 28, 2015, diaconalministries. com/wp/wp-content/uploads/2014/01/Guidelines-for-Benevolence-1.pdf.

6. Adapted from Jay Van Groningen, *Changing Times, New Approaches: A Handbook for Deacons* (Grand Rapids: CRC Publications, 1996), 88.

7. The idea of starting small and succeeding can be found in Roland Bunch, *Two Ears of Corn: A Guide to People-Centered Agricultural Improvement* (Oklahoma City: World Neighbors, 1982), 21–36.

8. "Nate," interview.

9. "Nate," interview.

Chapter 5: Ambassadors of Reconciliation

1. "Nate," interview by Katie Casselberry, November 3, 2014.

2. Adapted with permission from Timothy J. Keller, *Resources for Deacons: Love Expressed through Mercy Ministries* (Lawrenceville, GA: Christian Education and Publications, 1985), 56–58.

3. "Nate," interview.

Chapter 6: Rubber Meets the Road

1. Adapted with permission from Bill Raymond, *Building Transformational Relationships: A Manual for Mobilizing and Training Congregations and Volunteers* (Holland, MI: FaithWorks Consulting Service, 1999).

ACKNOWLEDGMENTS

This project is the result of the work, experiences, and encouragement of countless people, including:

Katie Casselberry, whose dedication, perseverance, and excellence on this project have gone more than the extra mile.

The many people whose voices and expertise shaped this project in fundamental ways, including Mark Bowers and Jerilyn Sanders of the Chalmers Center, as well as Randy Nabors, Gene Johnson, Shad Guinn, Shawn Janes, Jasper Reynolds, and Matt Seadore.

The team that worked tirelessly to get this project across the finish line, including Michael Briggs and Amy Kuenzel of the Chalmers Center, and our team at Moody Publishers, Duane Sherman, Pam Pugh, Adam Dalton, and Parker Hathaway.

The authors and organizations that generously allowed us to include or adapt their excellent resources as part of this project, including Amy Sherman, Bill Raymond, the Committee on Discipleship Ministries, Diaconal Ministries Canada, Redeemer Presbyterian Church (NYC), Think Tank, Inc., and the ACTS Collaborative.

The many church and ministry leaders who lent their experiences to this book, whether in the form of stories, policies, or insights, including Crystal Baxter, Hayden Blythe, Pamela Bolding, Ken Corr, Diane Croxton, Jeff Galley, Gretchen Kerr, Kirk Lithander, Dan Lowery, Andy Merrick, Michael Morris, Libby Myrin, Brian Petak, McKenna Raasch, Deb Richardson-Moore, Tim Ritter, Rick Sakaske, Chris Seaton, Kayla Siegman, Christy Taylor, Jeremy Taylor, Jeff Ward, Joan White, and the *Faith & Finances* facilitators and lead trainers across the country.

The Chalmers Center's Board of Directors, whose ongoing wisdom, encouragement, and leadership enable us to equip the church to empower people who are poor.

I, Steve, want to thank my family, many people at my church,

Highlands PCA, and students in my community development classes at Covenant College for praying for this project and me, especially over the past six months. In particular, I thank Mary, my wife and friend of 32 years, who deeply lives before the face of God. I am immensely grateful for her encouragement, empathy, and love.

I, Brian, want to thank my dear wife, Jill, for her unfailing support, encouragement, and sacrifice, without which this book would never have been completed. I also want to thank my three children, Jessica, Joshua, and Anna, for being totally on board with this book and all my work.

As always, we remain unendingly grateful for the grace and power of our Lord Jesus Christ. Only He can ultimately restore what is broken in us—and around us. He is making all things new, and it is a privilege to play some small part in His work in the world.

—Steve Corbett and Brian Fikkert

SUGGESTED RESOURCES

Online Resources

The following information and resources are available on the Chalmers Center's user portal.

Create an Account at: www.helpingwithouthurting.org/benevolence
Enter Access Code: walkwith

- Tool #1: "Developing Your Church's Benevolence Philosophy and Policies," a downloadable version of the questions in chapter 3.
- Tool #2: "Intake Form," a downloadable version of the form in chapter 4.
- Tool #3: "Action Plan," a downloadable version of the form in chapter 4.
- Tool #4: "Creating a Community Resource Directory," a downloadable version of the form in chapter 5.
- "Church Asset Mapping," the resource mentioned in chapter 5.
- Dr. Amy Sherman, *Establishing a Church-based Welfare-to-Work Mentoring Ministry: A Practical "How-To" Manual*. This guide provides excellent information on mobilizing individuals or teams of allies to walk alongside low-income people.
- Information about the following resources and training opportunities:

  Steve Corbett and Brian Fikkert, *When Helping Hurts: How to Alleviate Poverty without Hurting the Poor . . . and Yourself*

  Steve Corbett and Brian Fikkert, *When Helping Hurts: The Small Group Experience*

  Helping Without Hurting Seminar (DVD or digital video)

  Equipping Allies, from the Chalmers Center. This curriculum can be used to train allies or encouragers in your church.

Faith & Finances: A training opportunity that equips you to start a biblically integrated financial education ministry in your church

Work Life: A training opportunity that equips you to start a biblically integrated jobs preparedness ministry in your church

Additional Resources to Consider

- Diaconal Ministries Canada: Visit www.diaconalministries.com to explore excellent resources for deacons or other benevolence workers.

- Jay van Groningen, *Changing Times, New Approaches: A Handbook for Deacons*. This book provides guidance on benevolence work on a broader level, particularly for churches with diaconal structures.

- Timothy Keller, *Resources for Deacons: Love Expressed through Mercy Ministries*. Keller provides helpful guidance about benevolence work for churches, including information on walking with low-income people.

- Randy Nabors, *Merciful: The Opportunity and Challenge of Discipling the Poor Out of Poverty*. One of the most seasoned church leaders in the field of walking with low-income people, Nabors unpacks the biblical concept of mercy and what it means for fostering lasting change in the lives of the materially poor.

Keep exploring how you and your church
can foster lasting transformation in the
lives of the materially poor.

Explore all four resources:
When Helping Hurts
When Helping Hurts: The Small Group Experience
Helping Without Hurting in Short-Term Missions: Leader's Guide
Helping Without Hurting in Short-Term Missions: Participant's Gu